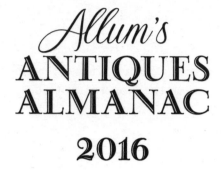

2016

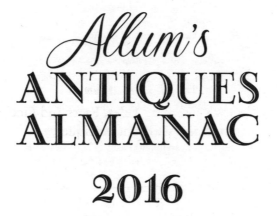

Allum's ANTIQUES ALMANAC 2016

An annual compendium of stories and facts from the world of art and antiques

MARC ALLUM

ICON

Published in the UK in 2015 by
Icon Books Ltd, Omnibus Business Centre,
39–41 North Road, London N7 9DP
email: info@iconbooks.com
www.iconbooks.com

Sold in the UK, Europe and Asia
by Faber & Faber Ltd, Bloomsbury House,
74–77 Great Russell Street,
London WC1B 3DA or their agents

Distributed in the UK, Europe and Asia
by TBS Ltd, TBS Distribution Centre, Colchester Road,
Frating Green, Colchester CO7 7DW

Distributed in Australia and New Zealand
by Allen & Unwin Pty Ltd,
PO Box 8500, 83 Alexander Street,
Crows Nest, NSW 2065

Distributed in South Africa by
Jonathan Ball, Office B4, The District,
41 Sir Lowry Road, Woodstock 7925

Distributed in India by Penguin Books India,
7th Floor, Infinity Tower – C, DLF Cyber City,
Gurgaon 122002, Haryana

Distributed in Canada by Publishers Group Canada,
76 Stafford Street, Unit 300
Toronto, Ontario M6J 2S1

ISBN: 978-184831-935-6

Typeset in Van Dijck by Marie Doherty

Printed and bound in the UK
by Clays Ltd, St Ives plc

Writing, to me, is simply thinking through my fingers
—Isaac Asimov

This book is dedicated to the many people who have afforded me the opportunities to be myself – thank you.

ABOUT THE AUTHOR

Marc Allum is an anachronism. Critics would say that he spends far too much time living in the past, but the simple truth is that he has found a career in antiques to be the most practical form of time-travel yet devised. So whatever epoch you choose, Marc will likely have something to say about it. Whether he's muzzle-loading a Kentucky long gun or soldering a 1960s amplifier, he will always be looking for an experience, an inroad, an insight. So, as this book goes to press, his garden will have been dug for the second time this year by the local archaeologists intent on finding traces of King Alfred's palace, which may be under his house. And as his work as a specialist on the BBC's *Antiques Roadshow* enters its eighteenth year, a position he considers both a love and a privilege, his pursuit of authorial time-shifting notoriety seems likely to continue.

CONTENTS

Contents

Contents

Contents

Contents

Contents

INTRODUCTION

Writing a time-sensitive almanac is a little like trying to prepare your tax return. It often leads to confusion, as, rather than accidentally attributing a train ticket to the wrong tax year, I have to keep thinking about whether the information I am collecting falls into the right literary year. Whereas the tax year runs from April to April and seems to be devilishly designed to hit all of us self-employed people with a bill straight after Christmas, my writing year is staggered, with the idea of being both retrospective and forward-thinking while still allowing *Allum's Antiques Almanac* to be out in time for Christmas – emblazoned with next year's date. It's rather like the magazine deadlines I often work to, when I find myself looking at Victorian Christmas decorations in August and the magazines are busily roasting turkeys and decorating cottages under sunny skies as their festive copy deadlines approach. In my case, stories eagerly jostle for position in the final 'cut' as I discard some lesser tales in favour of others that sound more alluring. It's frustrating, but I'm continually faced with any number of pieces that I wish I could have written about – particularly past gems that surface while I am gathering current material – yet, you will notice that I have a knack of weaving in the two, both past and present, in order that I can satisfy both my own curiosity and the desire to include even more macabre, extraordinary and price-busting news, anecdotes and gossip. It's the eternal collector's conundrum, the desire to want it all but, for the sake of one's own sanity, the need to be selective and keep only certain pieces. In essence, each *Allum's Almanac* is exactly that: another collection, another way of selfishly indulging my main passion.

This being the second volume, and given the experience gained in writing the 2015 edition, I'm hoping that my propensity for gathering such information has been honed somewhat and is working more efficiently. In time, the *Almanac* will undoubtedly serve as a kind of quirky barometer, a measure of market trends and fashion, the bevelled glass tapped out of curiosity to see whether the needle favours stormy or changeable, rather than being regarded as a dry, number-crunching bean-counter's bible. This is a book based on passion, for there is little in the way of science in this captivating and sometimes odd world. This is not a technical manual about antiques – you won't learn how to conquer the art market by reading this book. This is, plain and simple, my whim, my love, a shameless, thought-provoking personal expedition through the Himalayas of the art market wearing wholly unsuitable boots.

I'm often asked 'where do you get all the stories from?'

It's a good question. Trade publications, friends in bars, other auctioneers, chance meetings with obsessive collectors, chats with museum curators; there are too many sources to mention, each slavishly logged in my ever-enquiring head, each one a step closer to the summit, but a gentle ascent nevertheless, rather than an oxygen-starved battle against the elements, for compiling *Allum's Antiques Almanac* is actually an enjoyable experience that takes me closer to those realms of the market that still make me marvel ... how lucky I am. Enjoy!

Feeling Constable?

Art is the most intense mode of
individualism that the world has known
—OSCAR WILDE

Did you know that Salisbury is the only city in Wiltshire? Just the sort of fact that you might find useful at the local pub quiz; but, armed with an assignment by county magazine *Wiltshire Life*, I found myself on a cold, windy winter's day being buffeted around the old Iron Age earthworks of Old Sarum, just outside the historic city of Salisbury, with that fact foremost in my mind. It's a job I love, visiting a different Wiltshire settlement every month, wandering around extracting strange idiosyncratic information on history, customs, craftsmen ... and of course antiques. My remit is pretty lax and I enjoy chatting with locals, brazenly requesting admission to odd places and getting to know Wiltshire better, in what can only be described as 'an antique lover's peregrination in God's own county' (with apologies to Hogarth).

Salisbury, with its great 13th-century cathedral, is of course a historic place. Its origins at Old Sarum span several millennia and the medieval fortified town and castle that grew up within the Iron Age ramparts would have certainly been a gem, had they not been demolished and relocated to the plain below in what we now know as the city. The famous English painter John Constable (1776–1837) would have seen it in much the same way as I did, and his sketches attest to that. However, it's his paintings of the cathedral itself that perhaps epitomise his quintessentially English style. Constable images have become part of our romantic notion of what Britain looked like in the late 18th and early 19th century – the iconic *The Hay Wain*, an image which hung above my grandmother's fireplace, will be for ever indelibly burnt on to the art history timeline of my life.

Like many great artists, he was also much copied, so perhaps it was of little surprise to see that an oil sketch which appeared at a Christie's sale in 2013, and which closely resembled Constable's masterpiece *Salisbury Cathedral from the Meadows*, was attributed to a follower. You've probably guessed where this is going … valued at £500, it was knocked down for £3,500. Subsequent cleaning by the new owner and verification by a leading authority on Constable then propelled it into a different league when it was confirmed to be a preparatory sketch for that monumental picture, which is held by the Tate.

The study in question had previously been in the collection of the Hambleden family and was sold off as part of the contents of Hambleden Manor in 2007. After the 2013 sale it was re-offered by Sotheby's with a £2 million estimate and sold – inclusive of commission – for a whopping

£3.4 million! Quite a tidy profit, rewarding a person who presumably backed a hunch. However, this too seems relatively good value when you look at the £23.1 million paid by the Tate and four other galleries to keep the finished work (it was originally loaned to the London gallery some 30 years ago). This private arrangement prevents the picture from ever leaving the country, ensuring it will always be on public display; however, most pundits agree that it would certainly have realised much more had it been put on the open market.

London Calling

What do London Bridge and a corkscrew have in common? Firstly – before I answer that – it's probably a good idea to give you some history. It's thought, although not conclusively proven, that a bridge has spanned the Thames at London since at least Roman times. In fact, London would not have evolved as it did had it not been for a succession of bridges. Prior to this, the very different river landscape with its marshy banks would have been forded or perhaps traversed by boats, perhaps beyond the tidal reach.

After the Romans departed, Londinium fell into a state

of disrepair and was abandoned. The bridge would have suffered a similar fate but several subsequent early medieval bridges built by the Saxon kings would have become important strategic elements of the now re-established post-Roman settlements of London and Southwark. Evidence of a bridge apparently exists in a Saxon record.

The bridge was rebuilt by King William I after the Norman conquest of 1066 and then subsequently destroyed by a tornado some 30 years later. The last wooden bridge was finally built in 1163 and was managed by the 'Brethren of the Bridge', a monastic guild established by Henry II.

However, the bridge that we all associate most with the famous Thames crossing is the 'old' medieval London Bridge, a precarious-looking structure of nineteen asymmetrical stone arches with a central drawbridge, bristling with overhanging shops, dwellings and latrines. The infamous Traitor's Gate at the southern end, which used to display a gory collection of decapitated heads from executed treasonous individuals, can clearly be seen in Claes Van Visscher's engraving of 1616. Begun in 1209 and demolished in 1831, it was an incredible construction which morphed throughout its 600-year history into a legendary landmark. However, its existence was eventually compromised by its poor structural condition, its detrimental effect on the flow of the Thames and its restrictive effect on shipping, combined with its inability to cope with the large volume of traffic needing to cross the river. The new bridge, designed by John Rennie, was begun in 1824 and opened in 1831. It cost £2.5 million, the equivalent of £198 million today.

Most of us are familiar with the story of the American oil magnate Robert P. McCulloch's purchase of London Bridge in 1968, when it was decided to replace Rennie's granite monster with a more modern construction. The replacement bridge was opened in 1973 by the Queen. However, the idea that McCulloch thought he was buying the more picturesque Tower Bridge seems to be little more than an urban myth. The bridge is now located at Lake Havasu City in Arizona.

Given the enormity of these past constructions it seems likely that parts of them might still exist, and furthermore that souvenirs of their demise might also have been created. Not surprisingly, I have a bit of a passion for tracking down such artefacts and have a collected a few interesting examples over the years. These include part of a beam from the Norman keep of the Tower of London, bookends fashioned from the stone of the Houses of Parliament – after being bombed by the Luftwaffe – and a box made from part of a wooden pile from the 'old' London Bridge. It turned out that after 600 years the wooden piles that the bridge was built upon were in amazingly good condition.

A quick search around the internet also revealed the

whereabouts of several original parts of the 'old' bridge, including stone niches: two in the gardens of Victoria Park in East London, one in the quadrangle of Guy's Hospital, and another in the garden of Courtlands, a development of flats in East Sheen, built on the former grounds of a country house. There was once another niche here too, sadly now disappeared.

Much of this material dates from the 18th century and stemmed from changes to the bridge. There are also other pieces of masonry from the medieval bridge at the church of St Magnus the Martyr – designed by Sir Christopher Wren – and apparently at Kew Gardens too. So, that's the history lesson done. No doubt plenty of other stone is incorporated within the 19th century buildings of London, yet it's the smaller, quirky souvenirs that myself and others collectors tend to pursue, and that's where the story of the corkscrew fits in.

Corkscrew collectors can be fairly fanatical. Large prices for rare examples are not uncommon at auction, indeed, I personally found one just a few months ago that realised just shy of £10,000 for a client. However, Essex-based auctioneers Reeman Dansie were somewhat surprised by the price of a previously unseen 19th-century model made by I. Ovenston of 72 Great Titchfield Street, London – an unusual-looking device formed of three bow-shaped pieces of metal, one of them engraved with the words:

Made from the Iron Shoe that was taken from a pillar
That was 656 Years in the Foundation of
Old London Bridge

It sold for £40,000!

✤⟊⟊⟊✤

Dog On

I bought my young daughter a book for Christmas. It's called *Crap Taxidermy*. Within the pages are a motley but often hilarious collection of what can only be described as a waste of life, because if any of the creatures therein were killed especially to be stuffed, the results do no justice to their appearance in life. Many, of course, were stuffed in the 19th century, and much of their shoddy appearance comes down to shrinkage and poor preservation; yet, as I travel the auction rooms, I often see sad-looking, moth-eaten examples of foxes, hares, game birds and fish that bear little resemblance to their previous selves. However, taxidermy seems to be as popular as ever and even the 'genre' featured in my daughter's book seems to have become a collecting field in its own right.

Recently, while trawling through auction catalogues

online, I came across a small Victorian stuffed dog in a case. Hansons in Derbyshire had pitched the estimate pretty low at £30–40 and given that the fashion is currently geared towards such odd items, I decided to keep an eye on it in the optimistic hope that I might stand a chance at £500–600. In the meantime I decided to look at a few stuffed canines to see just how many famous dogs had been preserved for posterity. Not surprisingly, there are quite a few, of which some of my favourites include Whiskey the Turnspit Dog in Abergavenny Museum, apparently the last of a now extinct small breed that used to trundle around in a wheel, rather like a hamster, providing the power to turn the kitchen spit!

Tring Museum in Hertfordshire houses an amazing collection of taxidermy, among which it has a unique collection of 88 *Canis familiaris*, or domesticated dogs. One of the most famous residents is the iconic greyhound Mick the Miller (1926–39) who, as one of his legendary feats, won nineteen races in a row.

Other famous canines include the many Russian space dogs. Laika, perhaps the best known, was the first animal to orbit the earth, in 1957, in Sputnik II. She unfortunately died only several hours into the mission from overheating – a fact that wasn't revealed until 2002, although her plight certainly changed the idea of sending non-recoverable animals into space. Needless to say, never having returned, she could not be stuffed. However, two other notable

'Muttniks', as the American press dubbed them, were Belka and Strelka, sent up on Sputnik V in 1960, accompanied by a veritable menagerie of mice, flies, rats and a rabbit. Belka and Strelka were the first earth-born creatures to return to earth alive from a space flight. Their taxidermic mortal remains are housed at the Memorial Museum of Astronautics in Moscow.

The more I looked, the more stuffed dogs I found. Owney the Postal Dog, a stray border terrier who was adopted by the Albany, New York Post Office in around 1888, became a famous mascot and covered over 150,000 miles accompanying the post until, apparently, he was shot for being aggressive, which it appears may well have been the subject of a dispute between workers and management. A commemorative stamp was issued for Owney in 2011 and he can be seen in the Smithsonian, where he took up residence in 1911.

Given our general predilection for dogs, they have always been very useful for appealing to the gentler side of human nature and their use as charitable collectors became fashionable in the 19th century. They would spend their time at large railway stations such as Paddington and Waterloo, with collection boxes attached to their backs, raising money for causes such as the orphans of railway workers killed in the more dangerous days of steam. Even after their deaths, several such animals were stuffed and mounted in glass cases to carry on collecting for charity. Famous examples include London Jack, who began his platform-plodding days in 1884. Despite a chequered history, he is now fully restored and can be seen in the Tring collection. Another is Laddie the Airedale, who is on display at the National Railway Museum in York.

As for the small Victorian dog I fancied? Well, it realised a hefty £2,200.

⁕⁕⁕

Warts and All

In his book *Anecdotes of Painting In England*, Horace Walpole famously claimed that Oliver Cromwell's instruction to the artist Peter Lely was:

> I desire you would use all your skill to paint your picture truly like me, and not flatter me at all; but remark all these roughnesses, pimples, warts, and everything as you see me. Otherwise, I will never pay a farthing for it.

This was published in 1764, quite some time after Cromwell's death, and the quote seems somewhat unsubstantiated. It is, however, the strongest candidate for the origin of the phrase 'warts and all', as there certainly seems to be no evidence at all that Cromwell ever uttered those *precise* words – and his life is amazingly well documented. His famous wart, however, has always been the subject of some debate.

Perhaps the most accurate portrait of Cromwell – and he obviously preferred an accurate portrayal – was by the artist Samuel Cooper. Portraiture expert and *Antiques Roadshow* specialist Philip Mould staged a wonderful exhibition of miniatures in 2013 in which Cooper's exquisite miniature of Cromwell was exhibited. I was lucky enough to stand nose to nose with this emotive image and marvel at the skill of, as Mould eloquently said, 'this great topographer of the human face'. (On his death, Cromwell's son made a visit to Cooper's studio to buy the miniature of his father and – so the story goes – Cooper demanded £100 instead of the usual £20, which Richard Cromwell duly paid.)

In Cooper's work, Cromwell's wart appears in all its glory – rather flaky-looking, in fact. Yet in other representations, particularly his death mask, the wart appears to be absent. Conjecture about this refers to embalming methods and also a documented story about the wart being 'historically' removed and later donated to the collection of the Society of Antiquaries. Although now long disappeared, it was by all accounts kept in a matchbox and taken to social gatherings by a secretary of the Society, to amuse guests.

In 1658, three years after his burial in Westminster Abbey, Cromwell was exhumed. As you can imagine, Charles II was not in a forgiving mood and with the restoration of the monarchy, Cromwell's body was taken to Tyburn and ritually executed. His skull was – according to tradition – stuck on a spike outside Westminster Hall, where it remained for 25 years. As to its whereabouts now, well, it's thought that the skull with the best claim was buried in 1960 in the courtyard of his old college, Sidney Sussex at Cambridge.

Where is this all leading? Well, I collect coffin plates. Among a varied selection are several pressed Victorian examples featuring angels, truncated columns and such like. One of my favourites is a large brass hand-engraved plaque for a Richard Smith Esq., who passed away in 1776. So I was rather intrigued to see that the opportunity to buy Oliver Cromwell's burial plaque was afoot at a Sotheby's English Literature and History Auction. Frankly, this was only a wishlist item as it was undoubtedly – to my mind – one of the most historic objects to surface on the market for some time. The gilt bronze plaque, beautifully engraved with his coat of arms, was apparently meant to lay on Cromwell's chest but was in fact put in a lead case within his lead anthropoid coffin. Obviously removed on his exhumation, the plate had passed through several generations of the Norfolke family before being acquired by the Harcourt family – famous antiquarian collectors – in the 19th century. The lack of precedence saw Sotheby's playing it safe with an estimate of £8,000–12,000 but that was soon surpassed on the way to a final total of £74,500. I think it was still cheap.

N.B. As a footnote to this piece, the coffin plate later featured on a new series – *Antiques Roadshow Detectives* – in which an escutcheon (a painted armorial banner) from Cromwell's funeral, arrived at Belton House for an episode of the *Roadshow*. It bore an inscription saying that it had been taken from Cromwell's coffin by a schoolboy. This was later dispelled within the programme; although this is held to have happened, that particular escutcheon still survives at Westminster School and is part of their 'folklore'. However, this one was proven to be of period and it is believed to be one of many that might have lined the procession route or hung at Somerset House where Cromwell's effigy was laid in state.

Interestingly, the inscription is 18th century and almost identical to the inscription on another surviving escutcheon in the Museum of London. One was also sold at Sotheby's in 2013, again bearing a similar inscription, suggesting that some enterprising cad in the 18th century acquired a few and annotated them all. In any case, this one made £4,000, despite being in very poor condition.

Black and White

I often moan about auction houses that don't publish estimates or, alternatively, post ridiculously low values in their catalogues. I appreciate that there might be some defence for this but I'm sure that the 'come get me estimate' is generally applied because it entices buyers into the room in the hope that's there's a bargain to be had; then again it can simply be sheer laziness and lack of knowledge (I'm sure that won't make me any friends!). Yet, from my own experience of buying at auction, something that I do on an almost weekly basis, I would be the first to admit that I rarely know what I'm going to pay until the bidding is in full swing. In reality, the auctioneer's estimate serves merely as an indicator of what it could be sold for, if no one else is interested. Of course, that's what all bidders hope: that no one else will bid against them, whereas the auctioneer hopes for both maximum commission and the vendor's satisfaction, and readily accepts a pat on the back if the estimate is surpassed, taking it to mean that they did a really good job – which they often do. Conversely, and for whatever reason, the estimate can be too high and the item can remain unsold. The problem is, estimating art is not a science, and as both a valuer and a buyer it has become a bit of a personal conundrum.

Unfortunately, things just aren't black and white, and

as I keenly pointed out in last year's *Almanac*, an area which continues to defy prediction is that of Chinese porcelain, particularly blue and white. Bidders at Taylor's Auctioneers of Montrose were recently treated to a not altogether uncommon spectacle when a lot comprising two Chinese vessels, one an unassuming ginger jar decorated with prunus, and another more interesting-looking candidate in the form of a moon flask, surpassed their £30–40 estimate to make £200,000! What value would I have put on it? Well, certainly more than £20–30 but nowhere near £200,000!

Holy Backfire!

Wikipedia lists no fewer than 356 'Holy' Batman exclamations used by the superhero or his sidekick Robin in the 1960s series. I'm not sure how comprehensive or accurate this list is but a few of my favourites are 'Holy hole in a donut', 'Holy uncanny photographic mental processes' and 'Holy interplanetary yardstick'.

I can sense you wondering where my Batman claim to fame is coming from, and yes, I do have one. It happened some years ago when I was filming an *Antiques Roadshow* at the Gaydon Motor Museum in Warwickshire. One of the cars on loan to the collection just happened to be a Batmobile. Although at the time I was dressed more like Batman's arch enemy the Joker in an orange tartan suit, the curator very kindly let me sit behind the wheel of this famous car to pose for a photograph.

There are many myths and stories surrounding the Batmobiles constructed for the series but essentially four were made. #1 was the car used for filming and was based upon an incredible-looking concept car called the Lincoln Futura. Built in 1955 by Ford at a cost of $250,000, it was acquired by George Barris of Barris Kustom City, the legendary television and film car constructor, for just $1 in the 1960s. So the story goes, when approached by 20th Century Fox to produce a car for the new Batman series, he had only three weeks to do so and used the Futura as the basis to pull off his iconic automotive coup.

Given the success of the series it became patently obvious that they needed more cars to tour the States on promotional runs. Three moulds were taken from the original #1 and based on extended Ford Galaxie chassis. They all had their differences but the #2, #3 and #4 are all well documented. There appears to be some evidence that one of the other cars may have been used in filming but it's generally assumed that they were not used on set. It was one of these three contemporary replicas that I had the pleasure of sitting in, although I can't remember which one!

The original #1 was sold by Barris in 2013 for £2.4 million. However, it was with some interest that I noticed another Batmobile that had recently come up for sale. Altogether less futuristic and far more rounded, it had been built by a fan using a 1955 Oldsmobile, and aimed to replicate the look of the vehicle seen in the comic books of the 1940s and '50s. The car, finished in 1963, had been forgotten but came to the market fully restored. It realised £90,000 when offered by Heritage Auctions.

✳❧✦❧✳

Baltic Beauty

I'm often asked how you tell real amber from the various fake plastic and man-made resin examples. There are several tests you can do but first it's probably worth explaining what amber actually is. It is often mistakenly called 'sap' but amber is in fact derived from the resin that forms below the bark of a tree, rather than the sap which flows through the heartwood. Resin is the substance of the natural self-repairing process that protects a damaged tree when, for example, it loses a branch in a storm. The resin contains various chemicals such as succinic acid (which has various applications) and terpenes, which are particularly prevalent in pine resin. For a few years I lived in an area of southern France known as Les Landes, where thousands of acres of previously sandy and swampy land were re-adapted in Napoleon's era as large pine forests, expressly to extract resin and turpentine on a large scale. As most people know, it has a very characteristic strong smell and that's why pine forests can be quite pungent. The amber, which gets locked in geological strata, is formed by the process of the terpenes breaking down and leaving the resin. This can take millions of years. Immature amber, in which the process is incomplete, is called copal. Copal tends to behave much like its man-made look-a-likes when subjected to the same tests.

Such tests include tasting (make sure you clean your test sample first before licking!). The taste is subtle, more of a sensation than a strong reaction, as opposed to the distinctly chemical taste of man-made materials. Amber also floats in salt water – that's why it's commonly found on beaches, particularly in the Baltic, where pieces are liberated from their undersea strata during storms. To see if a sample floats, mix one part salt to two parts water and test accordingly. Copal sinks.

Amber doesn't melt, unlike polymer and plastic imitations, which when burnt also give off horrible acrid fumes. Amber burns with a pleasant pine-like smell; that's why it was used as incense. However, this is an invasive way to test an object. Rubbing real amber vigorously on wool will also give it a static charge so that it will attract small pieces of paper or hair towards it (a test that I've found is not always that reliable!).

Amber prices continue to be buoyant (if you'll excuse the pun) and I was interested to see that a large piece weighing a hefty 47oz (1,346g) had been sold by the Berlin auctioneers Kloss. The huge chunk was inscribed in ink by Alfred Lange and dated 1926. He later became dean of Freiberg University of Mining and Technology, hence the obvious interest in such a specimen. It had been found at Gross Moellen on the shore of the Baltic Sea. Amber is always popular in the Asian markets, as it traditionally has medicinal qualities in some cultures. This helped push it to a remarkable £25,600!

✻✥☙🙢☙✥✻

Rivet Rivet

I love riveted ceramics. The more metal rivets the merrier – and not only rivets: odd-looking lead repairs on handles and spouts, replacement tin handles on 18th-century Chinese tankards, all such idiosyncrasies of an object's life can have their own field of interest among collectors. The downside is that unless you have a penchant for such things, your riveted ceramics will generally be worth a lot less than a perfect example – a benefit for the collector rather than the vendor. However, the mere act of riveting suggests that such items were valued beyond their monetary worth and that was almost certainly the case with a large Qianlong famille rose vase that was recently offered by Toovey's Auctioneers in West Sussex. The neck of the vase had quite a few staples around the damaged rim – a pity for such a good-looking vase; this was probably why Toovey's decided to give it a well-tempered estimate of £10,000–20,000. In the end it seemed to make little difference as it was knocked down to one of a bank of telephone bidders, apparently a client in Hong Kong, for a far more riveting £520,000.

Jamaica Rum

On 7 June 1692, Jamaica was hit by a massive earthquake. The city of Port Royal, a vibrant trading centre and the biggest port in the West Indies, was destroyed. Prior to this it had garnered a fearsome reputation as the base of priva-teers and pirates. Founded by the Spanish in 1518, it was captured by the English in 1655 and proved an important strategic base in the Caribbean. Built on an island within the large bay opposite Kingston, the city was constructed on sand and as the earthquake struck it was literally sucked into the sea. Inhabited by around 6,500 people, it's thought that around 2,000 died immediately – mainly drowned and sucked into the liquefied sand. A tsunami ensued and various other parts of the island suffered great damage too. In the aftermath of the quake around 3,000 more people died through injury and starvation. At the time, commentators said that it was divine retribution for its sinful reputation. First-hand accounts sound horrific, with ships carried aloft over the buildings and sunk all around. Looting and general chaos followed and the city lost its importance as the main focus of Jamaica's trading centre.

So, armed with a potted history of this catastrophic event, it's probably easy to understand why rare objects associated with the pre-earthquake period are much sought after by collectors. One such lot recently appeared for sale at Shape's Auctioneers in Edinburgh, comprising two tortoiseshell combs and cases. They were not in the best condition but were clearly decorated with plant and animal life typical of the West Indies; they were also marked and dated 'Jamaica 1671'. In 2012 Bonhams sold two similar combs; their extensive catalogue description referred to them as 'wig' combs, one with fine teeth for removing lice. There are other examples in collections, including one in the Victoria & Albert Museum, but the Bonhams examples,

Print showing Port Royal and Kingston harbours.

dated 1693, were thought to have belonged to the infamous Henry Morgan, pirate and Lieutenant-Governor of Jamaica. They were apparently given as a present to Sir William Coventry. Ascribed to the only registered comb-maker of the period on Jamaica – Paul Bennett – they made a hefty £23,750. Although lacking in such a provenance, the two combs sold by Shapes were perhaps a little bit undercooked on an estimate of £70–100. They finally realised £1,700.

Lost Chaney

Every *Antiques Almanac* I write will naturally have to revisit certain areas of the market, simply because, year in, year out, records in certain genres will be superseded through the discovery of rare items or the deeper pockets of ever more determined collectors. I've previously covered film posters but on this occasion it's interesting to note that the latest record-breaker is for a film that doesn't exist, at least not any more. *London After Midnight* was a silent horror/mystery film made by Metro-Goldwyn-Mayer in 1927. Also known as *The Hypnotist*, it was based on a story of the same name and starred Lon Chaney. Known as the 'Man of a Thousand Faces', he was famous for his trademark make-up box which allowed him to play multiple characters. The film received mixed reviews at the time but was relatively successful; alas, no copies of it actually survive. The last known print was lost in a vault fire at MGM in 1967. As a result, it remains one of the most eagerly sought-after films in cinematic history.

The poster, of course, also has an iconic status among collectors, not just because of the film's history and loss, but the fact that this particular poster, recently offered by Heritage Auctions, is thought to be the only one in existence. Despite film posters being sold for higher amounts (one of only four known examples of a *Metropolis* poster was sold by Reel Posters for £390,000), *London After Midnight* realised a record for auction at £318,665. Perhaps one day, a copy of the film will surface in some dusty vault ...

❧❧❧

Mug Shot

House clearances can be an auctioneer's dream. Often, depending on the state of the house, it's not always clear what's in them until the property is emptied and the contents taken to the saleroom and sorted out. It was a job I used to enjoy when I was a younger auctioneer: that sense of discovery as you rifled through the mountains of boxes, accidentally tipping sugar all over the place as you realised the carriers had packed the entire contents of the kitchen, complete with all the food ...

No doubt Thomson Roddick Auctioneers in Dumfries had a similar experience when they spotted a little 19th-century printed Staffordshire mug in a local house clearance. Like many unassuming objects, it took a keen eye to spot the subject matter, a meagrely executed scene of a family on a shoreline, a ship in the distance, with the slightly smudged words above: 'Emigrants to Australia'. It's here that such a humble artefact takes on a new meaning. A small verse also accompanied the image of a distressed mother, perhaps seeing off her children: 'Now boys and girls don't let him go, pelt him well with balls of snow.'

It was cracked and chipped but this made little difference to the interest from Australia and it was duly sold to a collector from Oz for £1,200.

❧❧❧

Triumphant

Exclusivity. It's a great word to describe the reason why collectors are sometimes prepared to pay large sums of money for what appear – to the average person – to be quite ordinary objects. Special Auction Services have a good reputation for their cherry-picked 'Toys for the Collector' sales, and this last year has been no exception. Firstly, there were the two lots of six rare first-series Dinky delivery vans dating from around 1934 and printed with advertising for companies such as Hornby, Oxo and Pickfords. They made hammer prices of £19,000 and £20,000. These were always going to be predictably high in value. Less valuable but arguably more interesting in its exclusivity was the box of one dozen Dinky Triumph 2000 saloons. These were made as a special order for dealerships to promote the launch of the new car in 1963. The toys are rare in their own right so the carton of twelve, sent from Standard-Triumph Sales Ltd to H.V. Eyles & Son of Abingdon, excited collectors enough to make it one of the most expensive lots of post-war die-cast cars to sell at auction. It realised a triumphant £9,200!

❧

Battle Orders

I have in my possession an interesting item. Attached to it is an engraved brass plaque. It reads 'Watch Chain Worn By Michael Andrew Burmester At The Battle of Waterloo 1815'. Burmester was a Staff Surgeon and in this bicentenary year of the Battle of Waterloo (2015 as I write this) it's a tangible link to this great historical event. Being an ardent fan of both Napoleon and Wellington, I have written about them several times in my previous books; yet, given the propensity for auction houses to mark significant anniversaries with specialist sales, there could be no doubt that several more fascinating artefacts would come out of the woodwork this year.

Dix Noonan Webb, who led with a pre-emptive charge of sorts, holding a themed auction early in the year, offered what I considered to be some very interesting artefacts.

Having filmed an attaché case some years ago that had apparently belonged to Napoleon, I was rather taken by a leather despatch case, captured by Captain John Crowther of the 7th Royal Fusiliers in 1812 – some years prior to the battle but crucial in its build-up – which had been intercepted in transit from Napoleon to Marshal Nicolas Soult in Spain. Having lived for many years in the Basque Country of southern France, the battles of the Peninsular War are historically familiar to me; my old Château was at one point a shelter for retreating French troops after the battle of Orthez in 1814, where Wellington narrowly escaped injury when some canister shot hit his sword hilt. Here, he defeated Soult and pushed the French troops back towards Mont-de-Marsan. The Dix Noonan leather bag, originally fitted with a lock and chain, had been sliced, perhaps by a sword, and contained an old note stating that the contents (which had been passed to Wellington) 'had much influence on the Peninsular War'. It sold for a slightly disappointing £7,000 on an £8,000–12,000 estimate. In the same sale was a wonderful hair bracelet fashioned from the tail of Wellington's famous horse Copenhagen, a memento owned by a female friend of the Duke, Lady Shelley. The integral gilt locket emblazoned with a 'W' also contained a lock of Wellington's hair. It failed to sell on a £4,000 bottom estimate, perhaps the casualty of a slightly over-ambitious reserve?

However, the succeeding sale at Bonhams, one of several other auction rooms taking advantage of the Waterloo anniversary, offered some wonderfully historic items. Among the many swords, medals and paintings were a few absolute gems including a gold Irish Freedom box made by Edward Murray of Dublin in 1827. Given to Lord Uxbridge and bearing the arms of Field Marshal Henry William Paget, 1st Marquess of Anglesey, who commanded 13,000 cavalry at the Battle of Waterloo, had eight or nine horses shot from under him and lost most of his leg to cannon shot, the box made an all-inclusive £100,900! This being quite a story in itself, I have written it up under 'Leg Man' (*page 84*).

Cock-a-Hoop

Good novelty silver always draws attention and none more so than the wonderful zoomorphic claret jugs of the 19th-century London silversmith Alexander Crichton. Apparently between 1881 and 1882 he created some 34 animal-shaped designs for glass and silver claret jugs. It's thought that many of these whimsical creations were inspired by Sir John Tenniel's illustrations for *Alice in Wonderland* and *Through the Looking Glass*. Unfortunately,

One of Sir John Tenniel's classic *Alice* illustrations.

Crichton went bankrupt during the recession of the early 1880s and it appears that some of his stock and designs were re-registered and over-stamped.

Most commonly occurring is the cockatoo. The bodies are blown glass, usually clear but sometimes in colours such as green and cranberry; some even have enamelled bodies delicately decorated with feathers. The silver heads have glass eyes and the silver feet provide a sometimes slightly unstable base. Values vary according to condition and the type of crest but one was recently sold by Hansons Auctioneers for £7,000. They come with their crests either up or down and one with its 'crest up' had previously sold at Bonhams in 2013 for £15,000! Rarer examples include a Dodo, otter, sea lion and squirrel.

Even rarer are the creations of Sampson Mordan & Co., another company famed for their novelty enamelled Vesta cases, menu holders and propelling pencils. They too produced some stunning novelty claret jugs. A rare cockerel example, even with a broken beak and cracked body, recently made £9,200 at Byrne's Auctioneers but nothing lately has quite touched the enormous sum paid for one of their rarest creations – a kangaroo – which sold at Christie's in 2006, for a whopping all-inclusive price of £60,000. How novel is that?

❧❦❧

Launch Night

Last year's edition of *Allum's Antiques Almanac* was launched at the famous Garrick Club. Founded in 1813, it's one of London's most prestigious private members' clubs and is named after the great actor and manager David Garrick. Honoured as I was to grace its hallowed walls, I could only

imagine the plethora of esteemed actors, writers, play-
wrights and artists who had passed before me and I must
admit I felt rather humble. The art collection is wonderful
(you can search it on the club's website) and as I incorporated into my speech the works of luminaries such as Millais
and David Robert, which hung all around me, I literally had
to pinch myself!

It was a lovely evening and many of those attending
were obviously equally enthralled by the surroundings. One
guest commented on the various works of E.H. Shepard
(the illustrator of A.A. Milne's *Winnie-the-Pooh* books)
and how wonderful it was to come nose to nose with such
amazing illustrations – in the gents' toilets of all places!
A.A. Milne was in fact a 'devoted' member of the club and
left part of his estate to the institution. This meant that
the Garrick received royalties from *Winnie-the-Pooh*, and not
an inconsiderable amount. Disney had in fact been making
regular payments to the Garrick up until the club decided
to sell its interest in the estate in 2001 for a lump sum.
The money raised was used to establish a charitable trust
to encourage and help theatre, dance, music and literature.

Of course, many of us read *Winnie-the-Pooh* in our
younger years, or have perhaps read it to our children; I
keep a first edition at home. The simple pen and ink illustrations have a nostalgically memorable quality and at a recent
Sotheby's sale a number of highly sought-after original book

illustrations were offered at their New York and London rooms. Among them were a number of featured works from Beatrix Potter and Lewis Carroll and several originals from *Winnie-the-Pooh* and *The House at Pooh Corner*. Competition was fierce: '…and they all pulled together', an iconic image, made £75,000. 'So they got down off the gate', realised £85,000 and 'What had once been owl's home' sold for £39,655. However, the real star was 'Poohsticks', perhaps the most iconic of all and the frontispiece to *The House at Pooh Corner*. Who cannot picture Christopher Robin, Piglet and Pooh on the bridge? Who hasn't *played* Poohsticks, for that matter? When originally sold in 1928 at an exhibition of Shepard's work, it sold for 28 guineas. In 1975 it sold again, for £700 at Sotheby's. The other day it set a saleroom record for a book illustration at a massive £260,000. After all, there's only one …

Baby Doll

Over the years, the doll collectors' market has suffered from both the vagaries of the economy and mood swings in fashion. What once were the saleable staples of general toy and collectors' sales now seem to languish, largely unwanted by the average doll enthusiast – if indeed there are many! In the meantime, the market has been flooded with flouncy-looking, cheaply produced, synthetically dressed, look-a-like bisque-headed dolls, marketed as 'investment collectables' in the pages of Sunday supplements and relegated to boxes of mixed house clearance goods at the local auction rooms. Sad!

Yet, despite the depressed prices of the mass-produced Armand Marseille models that grace almost every general auction, there are still some bisque-headed examples so rare that at the top end of the market collectors will pay beyond what most people would consider reasonable for a doll. It was in the early 20th century that a much keener interest was being taken in children, their psychology and physiology, and this was echoed in the doll manufacturing industry where professorial academics were employed to model more realistic figures. The name Jumeau is synonymous with quality in 19th-century dolls and the appearance of their 'bébé' range in 1892 set higher standards in the industry, yet the 'Series Fantastique' ultimately moved the goalposts even higher in terms of expressive character dolls, with their faces set in a range of expression including laughing and scowling. Theriault's of Annapolis in Maryland recently offered a rare example in their New York sale and it sold for a premium-inclusive $285,000 (£190,000).

However, a few other such rarities had already surfaced

earlier in the year, setting previous records tumbling at Bonhams Auctioneers in Knightsbridge as three exceptionally good bisque dolls made by Kammer & Reinhardt made huge sums. 'Heinz', a character doll of a boy modelled after the nephew of the artist-professor Lewin-Funcke made a hefty £115,000. Another, of a girl, modelled again by the professor on one of his daughters, made a stunning £170,000; and the record-breaker – unsurpassed even by the Jumeau – was thought to be a unique portrait of a young girl, perhaps a test mould. Resplendent in straw boater and with plaited hair, she made a world record £242,500.

Cash Cow

Coins and medals have been selling particularly well in recent years. Whereas the hub of such sales was traditionally linked to London and specialist dealers and auctioneers such as Spink, the trend for running dedicated sales has gradually moved out into the provinces, with some startling results. According to the *Antiques Trade Gazette*, such sales have doubled in the UK in the last decade and the last year has been no exception, with some high-rolling results. A few notable examples include the Reddite Silver Crown sold by Spink. It takes its name from a Latin inscription around the edge, a new innovation at the time, which in 1663 was demonstrated to Charles II by Thomas Simon, the finest engraver of his time. Another version, known as the Petition, was also made and it's thought that no more than 30 were struck altogether. This example of the Reddite, which was last sold in 1950 for £360, made £330,000.

One of my favourite items came from Woolley & Wallis's sale of the Foley Collection which comprised around 600 medals dating from the 15th–17th century. It's traditionally quite unusual for collections like this to be sold outside of London but there was no apparent detriment to the prices achieved, proving the increasing strength of regional sale-rooms in this sector.

Another Thomas Simon item, the 'Naval Reward for Captains' is a 1653 gold medal that was awarded to captains and lower-ranking officers who served in the battle of Texel fought against the Dutch at the end of the First Dutch War. It's known that 80 were made and issued, of which eight or nine survive. Only three have appeared at auction since the Second World War and this one made an above-estimate £36,000. It's one I would have liked.

However, one of the largest sums to change hands was for an ancient coin, the gold aureus. Struck around 27–18BC, the coin, minted in the reign of Augustus Caesar, depicts him as Apollo in a stunning classical portrait. On the other side is the image of a heifer, again beautifully executed and hence its name the 'heifer-reverse aureus'. Of 22 known examples there are apparently just seven in private hands, which means that few ever come on to the market. This one, offered by Dix Noonan Webb, sold for £400,000.

❈❦❈

Black Beauty

As a guitar player, I'm always keen to see what's making the news on the musical instrument front. The appearance of Les Paul's legendary 'Black Beauty' guitar at Guernsey Auctions in New York was bound to set pulses racing for guitar collectors and aficionados alike. Paul's guitar, which he frequently modified and adapted, became the basis of his collaboration with Gibson, giving us perhaps one of the most famous guitars in history – the Gibson Les Paul. Expectations were high at the auction and the guitar carried no estimate. Previous record holders include Eric Clapton's Fender nicknamed 'Blackie', which sold for $959,500 in 2004; but the world record holder for a guitar at auction was Bob Dylan's sunburst Fender Stratocaster, a controversial guitar in that Dylan's appearance at the Fairport Folk Festival in 1965 with this instrument was regarded by many fans as a treacherous move from acoustic folk to electric rock. It sold for $965,000 in 2013. However, Black Beauty failed to ignite pre-sale anticipation to the same level and it sold to an undisclosed buyer for $335,000.

❧❧❧

Subject Matters

I've written before about the history and collectability of the Victoria Cross, Britain's highest military decoration for valour. I've also written, in last year's *Almanac*, about our nation's involvement in the Tibet Expedition of 1903–04. I now find myself combining a story about the two.

Lord Ashcroft's collection of Victoria Crosses is displayed on rotation at the Imperial War Museum in London. His generous donation of 189 VC medal groups and £5 million to build a new gallery means that the most comprehensive collection in the world now complements the 46 groups already held by the museum. Lord Ashcroft's unswerving endeavour to add to the collection also means that when any VCs come up for sale, he is likely to be bidding. It's here that the two threads of my previous writings come together in the recent sale of the medal that belonged to Colonel John Duncan Grant (1877–1967). As a lieutenant he had served in the 8th Gurkha Rifles in the Tibetan campaign in which he had shown great bravery by storming an artillery breach in the walls of the impenetrable-looking Gyantse Jong fortress. This he achieved with the aid of a single Gurkha. His VC was the last to be awarded before the First World War and was purchased by Lord Ashcroft for a commission-inclusive UK auction record of £408,000 (Morton & Eden).

Another acquisition for the collection came through the saleroom of Dix Noonan Webb. Awarded to Colonel Thomas Watson of the Royal Engineers, again a lieutenant at the time of the action, Watson was serving on the North West Frontier (India) in 1897, where he and a group of men from the East Kent Regiment and the Bengal Sappers & Miners were caught in a ferocious fight with local tribesmen in the Mahmund Valley. He suffered two severe wounds in the action and was praised by none other than Winston Churchill who was then a war correspondent attached to the relief column. It joined Lord Ashcroft's collection for a hammer price of £260,000.

Skip Cat

People love a good skip story and there are plenty of tall tales about valuable objects retrieved from skips outside decaying old houses. In truth, I've experienced it myself and I'm not averse to a bit of 'skip diving'. I will also always remember a couple on a routine valuation explaining to me how the skip outside their deceased elderly relative's house had been emptied every night, thus saving them a fortune in bills. I can feel myself wincing even now as they explained how the family had been missionaries in the 19th century and my imagination running riot as I envisaged hordes of local people filling up their car boots every night with rare tribal artefacts. Perhaps a little over-fanciful, but undoubtedly they had inadvertently disposed of some sale-able objects.

Such was a similar story that might have been attached to a small bronze cat had it not been for Penzance auction-eer David Lay. The 2,500-year-old Egyptian bronze leonine lovely had come from a house clearance but had apparently come close to being tossed in the skip. As it turned out, the cat had in fact belonged to a gentleman called Douglas Liddell, the managing director of the London coin, med-als and antiquities dealer Spink & Sons between 1976 and 1987. The cat, replete with two gold earrings, dated from around 700–500BC, making it 28th Dynasty. It had been authenticated by the British Museum and attracted a lot of press attention prior to the sale, no doubt aided by the 'skip' story! Estimated at £5,000–10,000, it went on to make a hefty £52,000!

Down Under

Few can imagine how harsh the conditions were for the first British settlers in Australia. The original convict transportees were often little more than petty thieves, prostitutes and conmen. Some would have no doubt been innocent of any crime at all, caught up within the harsh penal system that saw large-scale transportation as an effective way of increasing the British Empire. Among the many Australian convict sites that developed was Port Arthur on the island of Tasmania, known then as Van Diemen's Land. The ruins of the large stone prison buildings are a major tourist attraction on the Tasman peninsula and stand testament to the scale of the system. Originally, the site was a logging station, dating from around 1830. The prison gets its name from the Lt Governor, George Arthur. It was reputed to be the harshest and most inescapable prison in the Australian penal system, although it apparently pioneered

A 19th-century engraving of Port Arthur.

psychological correction techniques such as rewarding good behaviour with extra food portions, rather than relying on whippings and beatings. It was also the site of a juvenile prison where children as young as nine were incarcerated. The surrounding waters were, according to the establishment, infested by sharks but this did not stop some internees escaping. At the point known as Eaglehawk Neck, the isthmus on which the prison stood was connected by a narrow piece of land only thirty metres wide. As well as sentries and a fence it was protected by a 'dog line', a gruesome idea that featured up to eighteen half-starved dogs that were chained up and lived in barrels. They were supposedly an aid to the guards in case anyone tried to escape. The prison is now a World Heritage site.

Understandably, interest is high in material associated with such history; after all, it's relatively recent in the chronology of colonial expansion. We may joke about all Australians being descended from convicts but in reality the harsh truth about the way people were treated is just a matter of a few generations away, which makes it fresh in the historical record. The advent of photography in the 19th century means that we even have a pictorial record of the prison, including the convict ploughing teams and the guards. Unsurprisingly, the appearance of a 2ft-long black-painted truncheon at Wallis & Wallis created some interest. Faintly discernible on the truncheon was a 'VR' cipher for Victoria Regina and the letters 'VDL' for Van Diemen's Land. Given that the island was renamed in 1855, this fairly firmly dated it to between 1840 (the beginning of Victoria's reign) and 1855. It sold to an internet bidder for £1,300.

❈❧❀❦❀❧❈

Rock Steady

The pop memorabilia markets seem as buoyant as ever. To be honest, given the huge amount of Beatles memorabilia that seems to be available, I often wonder how it continuously tops the pop market. Not a year goes by when an iconic piece of Beatles memorabilia doesn't seem to surface and make a staggeringly high price – however, this year's round of sales has seen some ups and downs. One highlight was a complete set of *Abbey Road* 'out-take' photographs from the famous shoot by photographer Iain Macmillan. This set was signed and numbered 4/25, and came from the photographer's estate. It realised £180,000. Yet the star lot of the Tracks Auction sale – John Lennon's 1963 Gretsch 6120 guitar – failed to reach its £400,000 reserve. On the other hand, a plectrum used by Paul McCartney at a gig in Hull was sold for a monumental £4,000. A rare copy of *Mersey Beat*, Volume 1 No. 13, from the collection of the Cavern Club compère Bob Wooler, picturing Pete Best as the drummer, made £11,250.

Sun Stroke

January 8th, 2015 would have been Elvis Presley's 80th birthday. To coincide with this anniversary, Graceland Authenticated Auctions, which operates sales from his actual home, were able to offer an acetate of the King's first recording, the ballad 'My Happiness'. I'm not a big Elvis fan but it's fascinating to listen to this early recording, made in 1953 at Sun Studio, when Elvis was just eighteen years old. It's on YouTube and no one could deny that he certainly had talent at an early age. Apparently, the studio session cost $4. The acetate sold for $300,000, including commission.

❧❦❧

Fringe Benefits

Bonhams invariably offer some interesting material in their 'Entertainment' sales and their recent selection proved to be an enticing mix of the almost affordable and the eminently wearable. (Sacrilege, you might think, to wear a piece of clothing once owned by an iconic pop star, yet I do on occasion put on a suit once owned by Ringo Starr and thoroughly enjoy the conversation it inspires.) First up – and not unlike an example my mother used in the 1960s – was a green suede fringed shoulder bag that had belonged to Jimi Hendrix. It made £11,000. Having myself grown up on an aural diet of The Clash, the early death of their iconic frontman Joe Strummer in 2002 was a sad loss. It's that legendary status that perhaps helped his cotton 'bike jacket' achieve a sturdy £4,500. A good showing of personal items from The Who also saw Pete Townshend's early 1970s leather tour bag sell for £2,200, as well as John Entwistle's and Keith Moon's fur and suede coats, which made £1,000 each – perhaps a little too cheap for Moon's manteau.

Hat Trick

The Grateful Dead, known as 'the Dead' to die-hard fans, are one of the biggest legends in rock band history. Formed in 1965 in California, they became famous for their eclectic fusion of several musical genres including psychedelia, reggae and folk. Their legendary frontman, Jerry Garcia, unfortunately died of a heart attack in 1995, although his struggles with heroin, cocaine, alcohol and diabetes had brought him close to death on more than one occasion. Garcia was ranked thirteenth in *Rolling Stone* magazine's '100 Greatest Guitarists of All Time'. The band have sold some 35 million albums over the decades and the fans – known as 'Deadheads' – are commonly associated with a form of institutionalised American hippie culture. The most iconic image of Garcia is that taken by photographer Herb Greene and features him in the famous Stars and Stripes 'Captain Trips' top hat that he wore in 1966–67. It made £74,500 at a sale at Christie's, South Kensington.

Space Odyssey

The music industry is no stranger to controversy and one contentious offering in a recent Bonhams sale had interesting associations with the cover of the 1969 self-titled album by Blind Faith, a studio band with the members Steve Winwood, Eric Clapton and Ginger Baker. The cover of the album caused an outcry upon release, as it featured a nude eleven-year-old girl, called Mariora Goschen. She posed for the cover holding a silver lacquered model of a futuristic-looking spacecraft which was made by a jeweller at the Royal College of Art called Mick Milligan. The photographer, Bob Seidemann, summed up the concept of the cover in these words:

> To symbolize the achievement of human creativity and its expression through technology a space ship was the material object. To carry this new spore into the universe innocence would be the ideal bearer, a young girl, a girl as young as Shakespeare's Juliet. The space ship would be the fruit of the tree of knowledge and the girl, the fruit of the tree of life.

It was this model spacecraft that was offered for sale with an estimate of £6,000, which is exactly what it achieved.

I had in fact catalogued this item for a sale some fifteen

years ago and remember studying it with some interest. At the time, it sold for just a few hundred pounds, which, despite its controversial history, still proved to be a good investment.

Blind Vision

I was intrigued to see it reported that Tate Britain had recently acquired a very interesting portrait by the Moravian artist Martin Ferdinand Quadal (1736–1808), whose work can also be found in the Louvre. What was most interesting about this particular portrait was the subject, a blind flautist by the name of Henry Clemetshaw. He was the organist at Wakefield Parish Church for over 50 years, where a memorial tablet dated for his death in 1821, aged 68, bears the poignant inscription:

> Now like an organ robb'd of pipes and breath
> Its keys and stops are useless made by death
> Tho' mute and motionless in ruins laid;
> Yet when rebuilt, by more than mortal aid,
> This instrument, new voiced, and tuned, shall raise,
> To God its builder, hymns of endless praise.

Apparently, Clemetshaw lost his sight at the age of four but later became an accomplished musician. Depicted in the portrait, eyelids seemingly closed in concentration as he plays his one-key flute, it becomes touchingly apparent why. Dated 1777, Clemetshaw would have been 24 years of age when the portrait was executed. Although previously sold in the rooms of Dreweatts it was spotted by a curator from the Tate on the stand of Bagshawe Fine Art at the Chelsea Antiques Fair. Their delight in seeing it enter into a national collection was, by all accounts, complete.

Pound for Pound

As the political tides shifted and the English Civil War began, Charles I was forced to relocate his power base from London to Oxford. In doing so, he also set up a new mint to strike currency for those areas still under his command, one such coin being the 'Declaration Pound'. It was with some anticipation that Timothy Medhurst, auctioneer and coin specialist at Duke's of Dorchester was able to offer an example brought in by a private vendor. This large piece, minted in 1643, is over five centimetres across and by virtue of its size and importance declared the king's belief in his power as the absolute monarch. As history tells, this was not the case and he was beheaded within six years of the coin being struck, found guilty of treason by the 59 judges who sat at his trial and signed his death warrant. Incidentally, several who died prior to the restoration of the monarchy in 1660 were later dug up and ritually executed for their part in the regicide of the king, their heads displayed on spikes at Westminster Hall. The rarity and pivotal importance of such a coin in a turbulent period of English history was always going to make it a well-contended lot and this was borne out on the day, when it made an all-inclusive price of £56,120. Said auctioneer Timothy Medhurst: 'It was one of the rarest coins I've ever handled and it was an honour to do so.'

Freak Show

My predilection for the curious is common knowledge, so I was quite interested when I saw that Salisbury Auctioneers Woolley & Wallis had a mermaid coming up for sale. As we know, mermaids don't actually exist but stories of them have been prevalent in most cultures for several millennia – especially those island nations with a strong seafaring history. It's these stories that have spawned a curious fascination with associated mermaid artefacts.

What is certain is that any ancient mariner would have firmly believed in their existence. In retrospect, we now know that they might have mistaken aquatic mammals such as manatees and dugongs. Yet some cultures – such as the Japanese – have an ancient tradition of mermaid folklore, and this created a demand for the manifestation of such creatures. Mermaids in Japanese art are in fact quite ugly, very unlike the beautiful half-woman, half-fish that we idealise in our culture. Known as *Ningyo* meaning 'human fish', they look very much like a cross between a fish and a monkey, which strangely enough is exactly what they are. The earliest specimens to arrive in Europe were cleverly fabricated amalgamations of just that: half a monkey stitched to a fish!

THE JAPANESE MERMAID.—[From a Sketch by Dr. Phillips, U.S.N.

Examples dating back to the 15th century can still be seen in Japanese shrines and no self-respecting cabinet of curiosities would have been without one in late medieval Europe. By the 18th and 19th centuries, 'sideshow' freaks had become big business – entrepreneurs had realised that they could be very lucrative. Trade relied on the public's tacit acceptance of some elaborate hoaxes, but people were often keen to see the famous examples touring the world. Perhaps one of the best known is the Feejee mermaid (also known as the Fiji or Fejee mermaid) which the American showman P.T. Barnum exploited to great financial benefit in the second half of the 19th century. It went off the radar sometime around 1880, apparently lost in a fire. However, the Woolley & Wallis example was an absolute dead ringer and serious interest meant that I was soon priced out of contention as the low estimate of £300–500 was quickly surpassed up to a hefty final total of £5,124!

In a Bind

Have you ever owned a book in which parts of the cover or spine were made out of other printed material? Even as a boy I remember peeling away at the edge of my copy of

Ivanhoe and peering down the gap on the spine to try and ascertain what was printed therein. Indeed, the recycling of old books, and other printed or handwritten material into newer volumes is a very old practice. With the advent of moveable type in the mid-15th century, many handwritten manuscripts were replaced with printed versions and therefore became redundant, their vellum pages used as 'binding waste'. This recycling of very old books can add much to their history. So it was with a hint of nostalgia for childhood spine-peeling that I noticed an interesting sale at Reiss & Sohn, antiquarian book auctioneers in Germany, in which two vellum leaves which had been used as packing in an old binding had turned out to date from the 9th century and were in fact parts of the Venerable Bede's commentary on the Gospel of St Mark. The tiny writing was thought to be 'in an early Carolingian minuscule script' and possibly produced around 850–880 in the German state of Hesse. These two once-discarded pages realised £15,000!

Princely Sum

There are many lesser-known maritime disasters and none more intriguing than those which promise great rewards to potential salvagers. The *Prince Frederick* was a Dutch-commissioned, Glasgow-built steam ship of just less than 3,000 tons. Built for the Stoomvaart Maatschappij Nederland (Netherlands Steamship Company) in 1882, she plied various routes as a cargo, mail and passenger ship. However, on 21 June 1890, she set sail from Amsterdam for Java and Indonesia with a cargo of the usual mail, some troops and a complement of passengers, but also with a very valuable cargo of 400,000 silver rijksdaalders (a coin minted from the 16th century onwards and known in the Netherlands as the 'national dollar').

As the ship entered the Bay of Biscay, she encountered dense fog and apparently slowed to half speed. A British ship, the *Marpessa*, was also in the area and despite both ships posting extra lookouts, the fog was so thick that the *Marpessa* struck the *Prince Frederick* amidships with literally no warning, almost cutting her in half. She sank within seven minutes, but the *Marpessa*, although badly damaged, stayed afloat and rescued most of the passengers and crew. Seven soldiers were unfortunately drowned.

There have been various searches for the ship but she has never been located. Final co-ordinates for her position have not proven totally accurate and it's thought she might lie up to 3,000 metres deep. The value of the cargo today is estimated by some to be as much as $600 million! I'm sure, with the potential rewards at stake, she will be located one day, but I was interested to see the recent sale of an item associated with the sinking: a Holland & Holland twelve-bore hammer gun offered by Holt's at their London sale, bearing a large engraved presentation plaque on the walnut stock inscribed from the Dutch Government and dedicated in recognition of help given by a Mr W. Montgomery. An interesting tangible reminder of this little-known disaster, it sold for an affordable £2,000.

✻✾❦✾✻

Bounty Hunter

When I think about it, I often wonder why I treated my toys so badly as a child. It's only now, when I see the huge prices paid for mint and pristine items, particularly my James Bond Aston Martin, all my UFO and Thunderbirds toys, my Joe 90 and Captain Scarlet die-casts, that I rue my destructiveness and boyish propensity for re-enacting miniature pile-ups! The other regret is that my father had a clever way of keeping my brother and me very happy by purchasing lots of second-hand toys out of the local linage ads. In this case, he would supplement our basic Scalextric set with sacks of older cars, accessories and track, which we would customise and recycle into an innovative array of lead-weighted high-speed dragsters – those vintage Bentleys and Alfa Romeos can now make hundreds of pounds. However, we had our fun and it's no use decrying the fact that they were all made to be played with. For those who were otherwise disposed or had parents who only allowed the best toys out on a Sunday, their boxed gems have made it through generations to become the future collectables. Other items perhaps made it by a different route: old shop stock never displayed or promotional variations languishing in a dealer's cupboard. What is certain is that these are the items that become the Holy Grails of obsessive collectors. Often, it's a nostalgic generational thing; big boys buying back their lost childhoods.

Historic pop concerts, certain influential books, groundbreaking films and cutting-edge fashion – we view such things as formative episodes in our lives, pushing us into new areas of experience, even moulding our future careers. I've found myself referring to *Star Wars* on numerous occasions and I've argued its influence on popular culture with many a peer. As a thirteen-year-old it had quite an effect on me. My imaginary love affair with Princess Leia fuelled many an adolescent dream and as my career path progressed down the antiques and collectables route, my interest in science fiction, toys and film stood me in good stead for a career in general auctioneering. Over the years, I've filmed and advised on many such items on the *Antiques Roadshow*, most recently handling one of perhaps only twelve TIE (twin ion engines) fighter helmets made for the original film. I valued it at around £50,000 and it took Fiona Bruce by surprise, causing a mild furore in the press as devout fans moaned about her jokingly calling it 'a bit of plastic'. It's a lot of money but highly illustrative of the levels such scarce memorabilia can achieve.

Another plastic *Star Wars* gem, which did rather well at Vectis Auctions, came from the collection of former UK Star Wars Fan Club Chairman, Craig Stevens. Originally made by Kenner in Ohio, USA, the varying range of original *Star Wars* figures attracts almost legendary attention. This one, a plastic depiction of the bounty hunter Boba Fett, a now iconic character who first appeared on film in *Star Wars Episode V: The Empire Strikes Back*, was actually a much rarer version made by Palitoy for the UK market. Whereas an original Kenner version of Boba Fett might realise $5,000 in pristine original packaging, this one, dating from 1980 – described as factory fresh and with the hanging slot still unpunched – rocketed (fans will get the pun) to a staggering £15,000! This is thought to be the highest amount yet paid for a *Star Wars* figure.

Rape and Pillage

As for the legacy of the Vikings, it's not all rape and pillage! Thanks to the very important local history where I live, some interesting objects have been found, including a wonderful bronze Viking stirrup now on display in Chippenham Museum. As for owning such fascinating artefacts, these gems are surprisingly not only the domain of museum collections; in fact, I keep a close eye on the best of such good archaeological items that are periodically offered for sale and I was particularly taken by a very fine example of a Viking drum or box brooch dating from around the same period as Guthrum and Alfred (9th century). Of exquisite quality and remarkable workmanship, this particular bronze brooch, offered by online auctioneers Timeline, retained much of its gilding, with a central bead surrounded by intricate designs of animals in 'Salins Style III'. It was catalogued as the 'property of a 19th-century collector; thence by descent' which is always a valuable draw for collectors. Keenly contested, the brooch surpassed its £20,000–30,000 estimate to make an inclusive £47,795. Who knows, perhaps we might find one in the back garden when we dig it up!

Benchmark

My brother Gordon is a really good artist. He was recently involved in a project to raise money for the National Literacy Trust's Books About Town initiative to help increase literacy levels among underprivileged children in the UK. Fifty literary-inspired benches, made in the form of open books, were decorated by a selection of renowned and lesser-known artists. Scattered across London for the summer, they were brought back together and auctioned off at the Southbank Centre. Among many of the high achievers on the day, my brother's BookBench – inspired by P.G. Wodehouse's Jeeves and Wooster – achieved the highest price of £9,500!

Modern First

The phenomenal rise in the value of modern first editions has been stratospheric over the last twenty years. What is also interesting is the enormous difference that the presence of an original dust jacket makes. The jackets themselves are fragile and, as we all know from experience, easily crease, tear and become dirty. In fact, if you think about it, they are not a good invention at all. However, it's this idiosyncrasy that has been particularly instrumental in making some sought-after editions with intact dust covers particularly rare. The market, however, is often prone to unpredictability and in 2012, when Bloomsbury Auctions sold a superlative collection from the library of South African writer, film and theatre critic Clive Hirschhorn, there were some notable failures – as well as some notable successes. His copy of F. Scott Fitzgerald's *The Great Gatsby* came in at a low estimate of £50,000, which is by no means a small amount; Evelyn Waugh's *A Handful of Dust* made a healthy £14,000, yet a first edition of Graham Greene's *Brighton Rock* failed to sell on a £40,000–50,000 estimate. With some dust jackets repaired, conjecture was that many collectors preferred them not to be restored. However, although below its predicted overall low estimate, the sale achieved £725,000!

In the last year – as ever – Ian Fleming's various James Bond novels have been selling well; a group sold by Christie's of New York had the extra added cachet of being linked to Josephine Hartford Bryce and her husband Ivar Bryce. Fleming went to Eton with Ivar, whose middle name was Felix, and who is said to be the model for his Felix Leiter character, Bond's CIA connection. A first edition of *Diamonds are Forever*, with a good dust jacket and inscribed 'To Jo who knows the main characters', made £12,750. A good 1955 copy of *Moonraker* dedicated to Ivar made a very healthy £22,315 and another dedicated to Jo – a 1960 first edition of *Goldfinger* – made £14,820.

At Sotheby's, a rare 1916 edition of James Joyce's *A Portrait of the Artist as a Young Man*, sporting a particularly good dust jacket with some minor restorations, realised just over £54,000. I was also taken with a copy of Evelyn Waugh's first novel *Decline and Fall*, a 1928 review copy – complete with an exceptional dust jacket designed by Waugh himself – which realised just over £7,000 at Swann's of New York. In the same sale, the striking cover might also have helped a 1930 first of Waugh's *Vile Bodies* make a record-breaking £9,585, the price on the spine just 7/6!

What, you might be thinking, do I have on my own bookshelves?

❧❦❧

Cabinet Maker

Its very concept is the origin of our museums and it is currently the trendiest historical reference in art and antiques – the cabinet of curiosities. Hijacked by artists and reinvented for the modern age, this form of collecting is popularly illustrated by the once renowned collections of wealthy royalty and aristocracy such as Rudolph II (1552–1612) Holy Roman Emperor, King of Hungary and alchemist-collector, and John Tradescant (1570s–1638), whose famous museum Tradescant's Ark formed the basis of the Ashmolean collection. The 'cabinet' could be a room or series of rooms, or a cabinet in the sense that we understand it, a table-top or freestanding cabinet on a stand that would reveal jewel-like marvels from antiquity and the natural world in a series of small drawers and behind ornate doors. These cabinets were particularly fine. Magnificently inlaid in semi-precious stones and tortoiseshell, the Rijksmuseum in Amsterdam has some superlative examples, including a small table-top example made around 1630 in Augsburg for the merchant and collector Duke August of Brunswick-Lüneberg. It's a wonder in itself.

So, given the rarity of such cabinets, I'm always fascinated to see an example come to auction, although I can only dream of owning one. Provenance is always a major factor in adding value; so too is the name of the original maker, and a mid-17th-century ebony table cabinet offered by Bonhams had both of these vital elements. Signed by Elias Boscher, this superb cabinet is beautifully decorated with Florentine pietra dura plaques from the Grand Ducal workshops and mounted with Augsburg silver gilt plaques. It's a labyrinth of drawers and secret compartments, over

40 in total, made to house an equally exotic collection of objects. Its provenance, dating back to the 1840s, formerly records it in the inventory of Ballyfin House, County Laois and it remained in the family until it was sold in 2006. Offered by Bonhams in that initial sale, it failed to make estimate and was sold post-sale for £375,000. On this more recent occasion it made bottom estimate at £400,000 — perhaps not as much as was expected, given the current enthusiasm for cabinets of curiosity.

Murder Most Horrid

It's a case that has fascinated people since the 19th century: who was Jack the Ripper? This infamous series of gruesome murders that took place over several months in 1888 in the Whitechapel area of London shocked both Victorian England and the wider world. Even today, the hideous and grisly nature of the murders holds a grim fascination. In 2014, after over a century of speculation, it was announced by 'armchair detective' Russell Edwards that the true identity of the murderer had finally been resolved and that a shawl found near the body of Ripper victim Catherine Eddowes had at last yielded vital DNA evidence that the

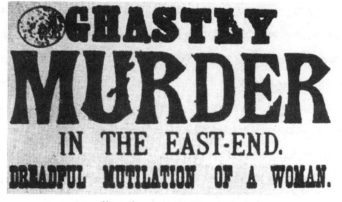

GHASTLY
MURDER
IN THE EAST-END.
DREADFUL MUTILATION OF A WOMAN.

Headline from an 1888 newspaper.

killer was 23-year-old Polish immigrant Aaron Kosminski, a barber. However, issues surrounding the accuracy of these results have since arisen and it seems unlikely, given the nature of these criticisms, that the myth of Jack the Ripper is ever going to be definitively resolved.

Directly connected to this story was the recent sale of objects that had belonged to police constable Edward Watkins. It was he who found the badly mutilated body of Catherine Eddowes, the woman thought to be the Ripper's fourth victim. Her body was found in Mitre Square in a spot where PC Watkins had apparently passed only some fourteen minutes earlier. The items, offered by J.P. Humbert of Towcester, had come from a vendor whose grandfather had purchased them directly from Watkins' widow in 1914. His number – 811 City – was clearly marked on the items, which included his truncheon, which sold for £3,950, the leather notebook cover (£4,450), his whistle, which would no doubt have been blown quite strenuously at the crime scene (£2,600) and his handcuffs (£6,420). These commission-inclusive prices far exceeded the expectations of the auctioneers but such interest amply illustrates the continued obsession among collectors with macabre historical events.

◆

Indian Takeaway

As I write I'm looking forward to the start of filming for the new series of the *Antiques Roadshow*. One of the highlights will almost certainly be an 'Indian Special', a celebration of Indian culture and, for many, an interesting insight into our past connections with this great and diverse nation. The show will take place at the amazing Hindu temple in Neasden, North London, which at the time of completion was the biggest temple of its type outside of India. This sparkling marble confection was inaugurated on 20 August 1995 by Pramukh Swami Maharaj, a sadhu or holy man, now 93 years old. The temple was carved in India using over 5,000 tonnes of limestone and marble shipped from Bulgaria and Italy and worked by over 1,500 masons. The

26,000 blocks were then shipped to the UK and assembled like a giant three-dimensional jigsaw puzzle. It cost £12 million which, given the effort, doesn't seem like bad value to me! Naturally, I'm looking forward to what the day might bring.

I have many Indian objects in the house. Favourites include a 19th-century sepia photograph of the Nawab Sir Muhammad Bahadur Khanji III taken around 1891 – resplendent in his finery, jewels and sword in hand. Another is an impressive Indian marble figure of a temple deity; these among many small bronzes and other interesting objects. So, although I'm fascinated by all manner of Indian objects, it's not necessarily a value issue, yet I was immediately attracted by the history of a cased set of jewels that came up for sale at Colchester auctioneers Reeman Dansie. It's one of those intriguing lots that – when you start to look into it – takes you on a journey. It was catalogued as:

An important diamond, emerald, ruby and seed pearl necklace from the Lahore Treasury, worn by Maharani Jindan Kaur (1817–1863), wife of Ranjit Singh, the Lion of the Punjab (1780–1839), Lahore, first half of the 19th century. Comprising six double-sided gold, enamel and gem set panels, two of which have been later converted to earrings, with rubies, emeralds and table cut diamonds to both sides with polychrome enamel detail and seed pearl fringe on a single row seed pearl necklace, in a fitted cloth covered case, the inside of the lid inscribed 'From The Collection of The Court of Lahore formed by HH The Maharajah Runjeet Singh & lastly worn by Her Highness The Late Maharanee Jeddan Kower'.

The precise cataloguing on the part of the auction house was spot on. Here in this one small lot is encapsulated a microcosm of the British cynicism and disregard for the cultures and countries that it dismantled and dominated in the worst of our imperialist past. The Lahore Treasury was fabled for its fabulous wealth. When the British dismantled the court in 1849–50 they systematically confiscated and took everything in it, auctioning off, in the Diwan-i-am (hall of audience) of the Lahore Fort, over a five-day sale, priceless jewels and royal regalia. The best was commandeered by the not-so-honourable East India Company, which took the Koh-i-Noor diamond and Timur Ruby (Spinel) and gave them to Queen Victoria. They're now in the British crown jewels. The box for the Reeman and Dansie set is also marked 'Frazer & Haws, from Garrard's, 31 Regent Street'; it's known that many jewels were boxed in Bombay, sent to England and sold through Garrard's. In fact, it's said that Garrard's still has a comprehensive list of the treasure which it has refused to release to historians. Whether this is true I am not certain but given that it was rumoured to be the biggest single treasure ever plundered there could be good reasons for keeping quiet, even this long after the event. Jewels were not the only items taken. Ranjit Singh's golden throne from Lahore, made between 1820 and 1830, can be seen in the Victoria & Albert Museum (collection number 2118(IS)).

So, what price this small part of a once immense and incalculable treasure? Well, others have come up for sale and elements of the great treasure are of course well-known in other museums and collections. In 2009 Bonhams sold an emerald and seed pearl necklace in an identical box for an all-inclusive £55,200. Reeman Dansee's set sold for £25,000. A small price for a somewhat sadly attributed but greatly connected piece of history.

⁂

Bacon and Eggs

Good usable dinner services can be quite cheap at auction. It's an apology I often have to peddle on routine valuations when I explain how familiar I am with the cost of assembling big services with large retail price tags and what they subsequently sell for at auction. Of course, there are exceptions and some antique services are naturally worth quite large amounts. However, if you are thinking of disposing of that unused 45-piece 1970s wedding present, don't get your hopes up too high. Interestingly, an initial glance through an issue of the pages of the *Antiques Trade Gazette* threw up some similar thoughts after I spotted a rather boring picture of a dinner service with a wide green border. To be honest I didn't even read the caption. It was only on a later, more thorough read that I saw it was a 1930s Cauldon service that had belonged to the famous painter Francis Bacon. Offered by Duke's of Dorchester, the service had come from Bacon's house and studio in Reece Mews, South Kensington and had apparently been given to Bacon by his sister Winifred. Consigned by the family of his friend John Edwards, the slightly punchy estimate of £10,000–15,000 was promoted as a relatively cheap way of owning a bit of Bacon. Items related to such interesting famous people usually carry additional value and cachet – this service would be worth around £150–200 at auction – so it's true to say that if you can't afford £42 million for a Bacon masterpiece (the record price paid last year for Bacon's portrait of George Dyer) the question of whether or not to put this in the dishwasher might seem quite trifling. However, it fell short of its estimate and sold for £5,800. A useful talking point at any arty dinner party!

Mum and Dad

A room hung with pictures is
a room hung with thoughts
—JOSHUA REYNOLDS

Norman Stansfield Cornish (1919–2014) was a former miner and artist, the last surviving member of the 'Pitman's Academy' of art. The community arts centre, more formally known as the Spennymoor Settlement, was founded in the town of Spennymoor, County Durham, in the 1930s, 'to encourage tolerant neighbourliness and voluntary social services and give its members opportunities for increasing their knowledge, widening their interests, and cultivating their creative powers in a friendly atmosphere'. The artists within the community worked in the tough environment of the mines but were able to learn to paint through publicly funded classes and Cornish quickly stood out as a talented painter and portraitist. He started work in the mines at the age of fourteen and, having established an art career, was able to become a full-time painter in 1966. He was a contemporary and friend of L.S. Lowry. Over the years his work has become increasingly desirable and his recent death has perhaps highlighted his position as an important exponent and recorder of everyday life, social history and the disappearing landscapes of the mining North East. Auctioneers

Anderson & Garland of Newcastle have somewhat of a reputation for selling such pictures and a good consignment of fourteen Spennymoor School works promised much for collectors of Northern art, including a superb self-portrait of Cornish. Estimated at £4,000–7,000, the room was in excitable mood, which was heightened by the presence of John Cornish, son of the late artist. His attendance proved somewhat emotional as it transpired that a previously concealed portrait of his mother had been revealed at the viewing on the back of the canvas, making it a double portrait. By all accounts, John Cornish inspected it as it was held up by the porter and announced to the room that it was indeed a portrait of his mother. Whether this made a significant difference to the price on the day is debatable; it was, however, a major bonus as this was undoubtedly the earliest known portrait of Norman's wife. The picture sold for £13,500.

In another sale held by Tennants Auctioneers of Leyburn, six works by Cornish were offered. One particularly appealing work of 'Two men and a whippet at a bar', crayon and chalk, made a record price for a work by the artist on paper, at £14,000. His loose, captivating style will surely appreciate in years to come.

Living Buddhas

We're all familiar with the ancient Egyptian form of mummification and what it entails (not entrails), but do you know about self-mummification? I was recently intrigued by news of the discovery of the thousand-year-old mummified body of a Buddhist monk found within a wooden lacquered statue of Buddha. The statue had been bought several decades before by a Dutch collector, who was unaware that it concealed the mortal remains of a self-mummified monk. It was only when conservation work was required in 1990 that the hidden contents of the Buddha were discovered.

Buddhist mummies are an ancient tradition and can be traced to most cultures that follow Buddhism, although the practice is seen by many Buddhists to contradict one of the essential doctrines in the religion – that of impermanence and the belief that existence is transient. Monks would often be mummified after death, preserved in a number of ways which included burying the bodies with desiccating agents, later to be exhumed and put on display.

The practice of self-mummification is an ancient form of self-inflicted bodily immortality. In Tibet and Japan, for instance, monks would practise a slow meditative descent into a form of ritual suicide in which they would gradually reduce the moisture in their own bodies by gradually starving themselves and taking powerful mixtures of laxatives such as urushi tea, made from the highly toxic 'Chinese lacquer tree'. They would then be buried in a box full of salt with an air tube and a bell which would be used to signal that they were still alive – or not. Another alternative would be incarceration in a very small stone room. One particularly striking modern example is the body of Luang Pho Daeng, who died in 1973. His body, complete with saffron robes and sunglasses, is displayed in a glass case in the Temple of Wat Khunaram on the island of Ko Samui in Thailand.

This *Sokushinbutsu* was made illegal in Japan in 1879 and it may be hard for most of us to even come close to understanding such an alien practice; however, one can't help harbouring a kind of macabre admiration for a person who can exhibit such incredible resolve and mind over matter to achieve such a state.

Anyway, the monk found in the Buddha is thought to be the only example of its type in the world and has now been thoroughly examined and tested by a number of different experts using CAT scans, radiocarbon dating and textile analysis. It's thought that he would have been aged between 30 and 50 years old at the time of death, and that the remains were 200 years old before they were put inside the statue. It was also found that the monk's organs had been removed and replaced with bundles of ancient paper printed with Chinese characters. Imagine, you buy a large Buddha and live with it for several decades before

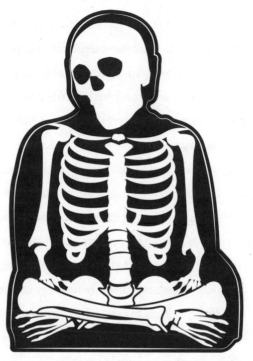

Illustration depicting the Buddha and its macabre contents.

you discover it contains a complete mummified monk. It's possibly one of the strangest stories I've heard this year.

❦

Storage Wars

It's a perpetual problem faced by auction houses – clients not collecting their purchases. Given the volumes often involved and the constant conveyor belt of goods coming in and out, it's very easy for storage to fill up; hence many salerooms impose charges on offenders. Having said that, I know from experience that it's very difficult to enforce such charges on good regular buyers, so as a rule I always try to pick up my purchases promptly and cause as little trouble as possible. However, recently I didn't behave as conscientiously as usual and a few days after buying a picture I rang up to apologise and to say that I was on my way to pick it up. 'No problem' was the answer, but after a half-hour drive I was greeted by the sight of one of the porters on his hands and knees, paintbrush in hand, halfway across a wet, newly painted saleroom floor. My picture was hanging on the wall opposite. I have to admit, it made me smile. No storage charges on this occasion.

⁂

Right Royal

This year it's been interesting to see that some famous Cartier pieces have come back on to the market – and it's been fascinating to see how they have fared, some years after their initial sale. Of course, provenance, glamour and superlative design can combine to produce startling results and when the Duchess of Windsor's jewels were offered for sale by Sotheby's Geneva in 1987, it was undoubtedly regarded as the sale of the century. In fact, I cherish the catalogues from the auction. Perhaps some of the most distinctive items in that sale were the panthère pieces for which Wallis Simpson accumulated seven specially ordered 'big cat' jewels over a twenty-year period, starting in 1948. At the time of the original sale, a tiger bracelet and matching clip realised £878,000, including the premium. It turned out that Andrew Lloyd Webber had purchased them for his then wife Sarah Brightman, in celebration of the massive success of *Phantom of the Opera*. Their recent resale by Brightman at Christie's Geneva did, it must be said, have some historical precedence for a good improvement in value. This can sometimes be difficult as people often get carried away at such landmark disposals. However, a panthère bracelet from the same sale, which had originally made just over £860,000, had resold at Sotheby's in 2010 for £4 million. Not a bad improvement. Brightman's lot didn't do quite as well and realised £1.78 million.

Conversely, jewels owned by HRH Princess Margaret seem not to have been such a good investment when sold by Christie's in 2006. Much vaunted, the original 800-lot sale was also a well-branded marketing operation; the hyped sale saw lots accompanied by authenticity material and some items even engraved especially for sale. Controversy ensued with accusations of a 'right royal sell-off', questions about the ownership of some items and the moral issues of selling the Queen's sister's personal and state possessions. However, the sale proceeded and many personal items found their way to new homes. Three such items were recently offered for sale by Fellowes auctioneers – again, all Cartier items. A diamond wristwatch dating from around 1911 realised £12,000. It had sold for £30,000 in 2006. A diamond bracelet worn to the premier of The Beatles' film *Help!* made £24,000. It had previously made £55,000. A diamond ring originally given to Mary, Duchess of York in 1893, made £16,000. It had made £48,000 at Christie's.

I don't think there's any particular moral here but it does go to prove the lure of hype and just how unpredictable the markets can be.

Love Tie

I love jewellery, but the opportunities for men to wear it are somewhat limited within the everyday bounds of what is considered reasonable in a working environment! So, I have a good selection of cufflinks (a couple of pairs that belonged to Elton John), various watches, plenty of rings, including various intaglios and a diamond monster that would have been worn by some flamboyant macaroni, a few watch chains for when I want to dandy it up with a waistcoat and a very varied selection of tie pins and clips. As fashion seems to be rather more casual at the moment, open necks are much more acceptable but there was a time when no self-respecting gentleman would have been seen without a necktie or cravat. I'm not a big one for cravats but I do like ties and I also like tie and cravat pins. There are countless different designs. Commonly occurring versions include foxes' heads with gem-set eyes, enamelled game birds, swords, coins, military badges, Masonic emblems and so on. But I recently saw one that I had never come across before. Made in gold, it resembled a square postbox with the word 'RUE' on the front – initials rather than the French, I imagine. This tiny box, intricately made with minute hinges, unfolded to reveal a small blue enamelled bird on a spring, rather like a jack-in-the-box. Although not mentioned in the auctioneer's description, I imagine the blue bird may have denoted happiness – an ancient symbol of springtime and joy. Perhaps this was given as a little keepsake, as jewellery often is. Most commonly occurring pins fall into the £100–200 price bracket at auction but this one was certainly going to be a little more expensive. Offered by Roseberys of West Norwood in London, it made a hammer price of £550.

From the Bridge

I've done a lot of lecturing on cruise ships over the years. On one particular Swedish line the ship's captain had an annoying early morning ritual of waking everybody up over the tannoy with an often humorous pronouncement 'from the bridge'. Despite many happy memories, I can't say that I've always enjoyed being on a cruise ship. Among the many skills needed to adapt to cruise ship living, I became extremely adept at countering the massive vibration of the side-thrusters by inserting lots of folded pieces of card between the fitted cabinets in the cabin – this in the vain hope of stopping the terrible noise from the ill-fitting fixtures. This would sometimes result in a kind of confetti when caught in a bad storm. Of course, jokes about the *Titanic* would always be on people's lips and sometimes there would even be a lecturer on board who specialised in talking about maritime disasters. This always worried me!

Humour aside, *Titanic* memorabilia still brings enormous prices at auction. In the last *Almanac*, I wrote of the extremely emotive experience with the violin from the Titanic that was sold for a million pounds by maritime auction specialists Henry Aldridge and sons of Devizes, and this year I filmed a programme for the *Antiques Roadshow* which took me on an interesting journey around Southampton tracing the life of Captain Arthur Rostron of the Cunard Ship RMS *Carpathia*, who steamed to the aid of the stricken ship, rescuing some 705 souls from the water. In the meantime, several auction records have been broken. Aldridge's have again provided the running for the most expensive items with the sale of the only surviving letter thought to have been written on the *Titanic*. The letter was penned by Esther Hart and her daughter Eva, a famous survivor who was aged seven at the time and who passed away in 1996; they were second-class passengers. Husband and father Benjamin Hart helped them into a lifeboat and was never seen again. Excerpts from the letter read:

> My Dear ones all. As you see it is Sunday afternoon and we are resting in the library after luncheon. I was very bad all day yesterday could not eat or drink and sick all the while, but today I have got over it …
>
> Tho they say this Ship does not roll on account of its size. Any how it rolls enough for me, I shall never forget it. It is very nice weather but awfully windy and cold…

Said Andrew Aldridge from the auctioneers, 'the importance of this legendary item cannot be overstated, being the only known surviving example of its type to have been written on that fateful day, surviving the sinking, and having belonged to such a well-known survivor.' It made a world record for a *Titanic*-related letter of £119,000.

STOP PRESS: Aldridge's have just sold one of only six or seven deckchairs originally picked up from the site of the *Titanic* sinking for £100,000. It's the second time it has passed through their hands.

⁂

Leg Man

Accounts of battles are commonly peppered with acts of great altruism heroism and selflessness. It seems that 'when the chips are down' or the going gets tough, people will stop at nothing to save others, or bravely battle on against all the odds. Waterloo was no exception. Although I have already dealt with the subject of the bicentenary of the battle, there was one particular story that I wanted to expand upon – a story that epitomises the popular brave and romantic image of a 19th-century military man.

Soon after, the site of the battle quickly became a major tourist attraction – as it still is today. Veterans offered their services as guides, a fact that reminds me of one of my greatest regrets, having many years ago narrowly missed the acquisition of a hand-coloured personal calling card once given by a veteran battlefield guide – c'est la vie! For most people, the battle itself is symbolised by the great

Lion's Mound, a large conical man-made hill topped by a huge lion on a stone plinth and finished in 1826 to commemorate where the Prince of Orange was knocked from his horse by a musket ball. It has over time become a universal symbol rather than a personal monument.

Back to the story. As you read in 'Battle Orders' (*page 30*), I outlined the sale of a gold box belonging to Lord Uxbridge. The story of his blasted leg is typical of one of those strange macabre yet fascinating tales of heroism coupled with a public obsession for the perverse – I suppose that's why I like the story myself! Lord Uxbridge commanded 13,000 Allied cavalry and 44 pieces of horse artillery at the Battle of Waterloo. Late on in the battle, after leading numerous charges and offensives, his leg was hit by some grapeshot which completely shattered the bone below his knee. This led

The Lion's Mound, Waterloo, Belgium.

to the famous account of an exchange between himself and the Duke of Wellington in which he apparently exclaimed 'By God, sir, I've lost my leg!' and to which Wellington replied 'By God, sir, so you have!'

This was not the only anecdotal report of the event, for on being taken back to his headquarters in the village of Waterloo – a house belonging to a M. Hyacinthe Joseph-Marie Paris – his leg was amputated, without any anaesthetic, by two surgeons, James Powell of the OMD (Ordnance Medical Division) and James Callander of the 7th Hussars. Unbelievably stoical and typically irreverent in a British upper-class humorous manner, Uxbridge made many quips about the situation, reportedly saying things such as 'I have had a pretty long run. I have been a beau these 47 years, and it would not be fair to cut the young men out any longer'. He even moaned that the surgical instruments seemed blunt and asked of one of his cavalry commanders, Sir Hussey Vivian, to inspect the amputated leg to ensure that it really wasn't a mistake to have it removed; he reported to Uxbridge that 'it was better off than on'.

M. Paris then asked if he could bury the leg in his garden and a stone was erected which read:

Here lies the Leg of the illustrious and valiant Earl Uxbridge, Lieutenant-General of His Britannic Majesty,

Commander in Chief of the English, Belgian and Dutch cavalry, wounded on the 18 June 1815 at the memorable battle of Waterloo, who, by his heroism, assisted in the triumph of the cause of mankind, gloriously decided by the resounding victory of the said day.

Apparently, visitors (i.e. tourists) would first be taken to the place of the amputation in the house, a blood-stained chair (although another story tells of Uxbridge returning with his sons and eating dinner from the *table* where the operation took place), before being shown the spot where the leg was buried. M. Paris and his descendants did very nicely out of the leg; it even attracted a visit from the King of Prussia and the Prince of Orange. However, in 1878 when a visit by Uxbridge's son took place, the bones were found to be on display, which caused a diplomatic furore and a demand from the Belgian ambassador that they be repatriated. The Paris family offered to sell the bones to the Uxbridges but the Uxbridges were understandably very upset by the whole incident. The bones were subsequently hidden and only resurfaced in 1934 in the study of the last, late M. Paris. His widow then burnt them in the central heating furnace, fearing a repeat of another incident. However, Lord Uxbridge's wooden leg and the trousers worn by him at the battle can be seen at his home Plas Newydd on Anglesey, which incidentally is the venue for an upcoming *Antiques Roadshow* — I can't wait! The surgical saw that removed his leg is preserved in the National Army Museum. It would be interesting to see just how sharp it is …

❧❀❧

Horse Play

I've come across quite a few interesting stories about horses and their exploits – particularly military. After all, they were for thousands of years the main form of transport of both civilians and the military, as well as the primary vehicle of attack in battle; consequently, millions have given up their lives in the service of their masters and countries. It was only recently that we filmed an *Antiques Roadshow* at Tredegar House near Newport, South Wales, the ancestral home of the Morgan family. There in the grounds is the grave of and memorial to Sir Briggs, a champion steeplechaser taken to Crimea and ridden by Godfrey Morgan in the Charge of the Light Brigade. By all accounts, his steeplechasing pedigree made him an excellent jumper and he cleared the Russian cannons during the charge. Morgan put his own survival down to Sir Briggs and this well-respected horse lived out his life at Tredegar for another twenty years.

Historic 'warhorses', as they are commonly known, are

given more respect than you might imagine and a recent article in *The Sunday Times* did lead me to do a little bit of research on the whereabouts of other trusty chargers. Again on the theme of Waterloo, the article outlined the case for the idea that Marengo – whose skeleton is preserved in the National Army Museum in Chelsea – is not Napoleon's grey Arab charger as stated, but an imposter. The popular story is that Napoleon's horse was captured at the Battle of Waterloo by William Henry Francis Petre, 11th Baron Petre, and brought back to England. He lived to the ripe old age of 38 and his preserved skeleton thereafter found its way to the museum. However, Gareth Glover, author and the treasurer of the Waterloo Association, has done extensive research and concludes in his book *Waterloo in 100 Objects* that no such horse existed and that he actually has a fake provenance.

What is certain is that the taxidermal horse in the Musée de L'Armée in Paris – Le Vizir – definitely was Napoleon's horse and was given to him in 1808 by Sultan Mahmud II. He has a brand of Napoleon's famous crowned 'N' on his left flank and even accompanied 'Boney' to his island prison of St Helena. The Duke of Wellington's famous warhorse, Copenhagen, ridden continually on the day of the battle for seventeen hours, is buried at the Duke's estate of Stratfield Saye. Apparently the Duke was asked if he would disinter Copenhagen so that his skeleton could be displayed alongside that of Marengo. He declined with the excuse that

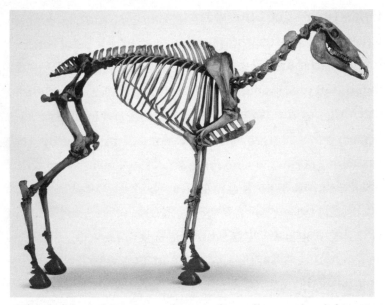

The skeleton of Marengo – but was he really Napoleon's horse?

he could not remember where he was buried – which, of course, was not true. A marble headstone marks the spot, having later been erected by the Duke's son, and reads:

Here Lies

COPENHAGEN

The Charger ridden by

THE DUKE OF WELLINGTON

The entire day at the

BATTLE OF WATERLOO.

Born 1808. Died 1836.

God's humbler instrument though meaner clay
Should share the glory of that glorious day.

Other Interesting Stuffed Horses

COMANCHE   After the slaughter of the Battle of Little Bighorn, the first reinforcements to arrive on the scene found only one living creature – a horse. Other animals had no doubt survived but had obviously been taken or had been spooked and run away. Comanche had been injured, sustaining seven gunshot wounds. He was heralded as the last living survivor of the battle and was nursed back to health. He became the honorary second-in-command of the US 7th Cavalry and after his death in 1890 he was preserved and exhibited at the 1893 Chicago World's Fair. He can now be seen at the Natural History Museum of the University of Kansas.

STREIFF   Streiff is the 400-year-old mount of King Gustav Adolphus of Sweden who was fatally shot at the Battle of Lützen in 1632; the horse was also fatally wounded but can be seen preserved in the Swedish Royal Armouries in Stockholm. Unlike the king.

LISETTE   This trusty charger was a favourite of Peter the Great and is credited with saving his life after she inadvertently jinked, causing a sniper's musket ball to miss the Tsar at the Battle of Poltava in 1709. Instead, it hit the saddle. Peter the Great was eternally grateful and spoilt the horse for the rest of her life. Lisette's remains can be seen in the Zoological Museum in St Petersburg.

Temple of Delights

I'm a big fan of antique architectural models, particularly examples from the Grand Tour. Among my array of bronze Arcs de Triomphe, marble Roman Forums and temples of Vesta there are some cork models. Why cork, you might wonder? As a modelling material it is actually quite practical and well-suited to representing ancient stone buildings. The art form, known as 'phelloplastik' from the Greek *phello* for cork, became popular in the 18th century as a way of supplying accurate architectural models of great temples and buildings to the Grand Tourists. Not only did they look wonderful, they were also light, making transport a little easier – fragility aside! The industry, mainly based in Naples and Rome, had several well-known specialists who supplied tourists and scholars alike. Sir John Soane (1753–1837), the great Neoclassical architect, had a model room populated by such examples and he also used them as teaching aids. One of the models in his collection is a 'to die for' cork representation of the Temple of Zeus at Paestum. Such fine scale examples were made by masters such as Augusto Rosa (1738–1784) Giovanni Altieri (1767–1790) and Domenico Padiglione and his sons. Padiglione was an employee at the Royal Museum in Naples and worked as their official model maker in the early 19th century. Attributed examples are of course very much more desirable and are must-have items for discerning Neoclassicists and collectors of Grand Tour memorabilia.

Sworders of Mountfitchet recently offered a good example of the Temple of Zeus at Paestum, which at 63cm long was an impressive size. Notoriously difficult to clean and often in less than perfect condition, the rather low catalogue estimate of £400–600 was soon surpassed to make a more fitting £25,000. That's £735 per architectural column!

$$\text{\small ❧}$$

Bird in the Hand

The attraction of good jewellery seems to be as enduring as ever. The ingenuity of designers and jewellers is immensely varied and there's not a week goes by that I don't spot an interesting variation on an old theme or something incredibly novel as I scan the pages of auction catalogues. There are also plenty of unique jewellery items around, which allow owners a sense of exclusivity. Couple this with the hidden language of jewels and they can make for a potent cocktail of clandestine intrigue. Certainly, there has also been a big rise in the interest surrounding 20th-century and in particular post-war jewellery design.

I am always pleased to see pieces by companies such as

Cartier, who have, throughout their history, maintained a sense of playfulness and humour in much of their work. Of course, this can be down to the demands and requirements of individual clients, but these quirky pieces were often reinventions of fashionable costume jewellery, albeit made in precious stones and metals.

During the Nazi occupation of Paris in the Second World War, Cartier created a quirky jewel that held great symbolism. The inhabitants of Paris referred to themselves as caged birds and in 1942 Jeanne Toussaint, the director of fine jewellery at Cartier, designed a pendant in the form of a caged bird. The coral, lapis and diamonds used in the design represented the colours of the French flag. At the end of the war another version was made with the cage door open. These are known as 'Liberation Brooches'. There are also other variations, but they rarely come up for sale. In 2007 Christie's Geneva sold a fine bird brooch with the words '1946 WILL BE BETTER' fashioned in gold as part of the surround beneath the coral-and-lapis-mounted singing bird. It made $7,921.

Post-war Cartier bird brooches dating from the 1950s and 1960s are among my favourite high fashion jewellery creations. Despite their value, they have an inverted ostentation, which only on closer inspection really belies their workmanship. Several have come on to the market in the last couple of years and they are highly sought after by collectors with an eye on the currently popular retro-fashion market. The best, to my mind, was an eccentric-looking duck fashioned from white agate with an emerald eye, sporting a Native American headdress with a coral-mounted war hammer poised behind his back. Quite unusual but great fun! It made £17,000 at Bearnes Hampton & Littlewood of Exeter in 2014. More recently, a little chalcedony sparrow made £4,500 at Bonhams; but a particularly fine, and quite comical, running goose with a turquoise body, set with diamonds, made a rather more hefty £23,500 at Clevedon Salerooms near Bristol. Quite simply, if you weren't careful, one could easily pass you by.

Wheels of Industry

There's a particular style of clock that has become increasingly collectable over the years. Known as 'industrial' novelty compendium clocks, their designs are based largely on technical apparatus, locomotives, boilers and buildings. No doubt part of the interest in them stems from a fascination for early technological and industrial innovation. Indeed, the variety of designs is quite amazing. Most herald from France. The 'compendium' aspect derives from the fact that most incorporate barometers and thermometers within their design, often loosely disguised as dials on equipment. The quality of the clocks can also be quite astounding – although, as in most areas, there are also 'poor man's versions' available. However, when they are good, they really stand out and the more unusual the designs the better. Slightly more common examples include large steam hammers, ship's wheels and vertical pumping engines; real rarities are the iron-clad battleships and locomotives. A few of my past favourites include a superb automaton loco sold by Fountaine's Auctioneers in Massachusetts in 2009, for just over $31,000. More recent examples feature a wonderful clock by the famous maker Jacques Ullmann, who had shops as far apart as Hong Kong, Shanghai, Paris and Vladivostok. Offered by auctioneers John Nicholson, an unrestored and very original clock in the form of a radial electric motor recently sold for £9,000. Another in the same sale and from the same source, in the form of a vertical piston engine, made £8,000.

❧⳥⳥❧

Roman Riches

It's one of the most enigmatic and controversial hoards to come to light in recent decades – the Sevso Treasure. When

I was in my twenties I knew a professional archaeological illustrator who had been commissioned to record and draw it in its entirety following its appearance around 1980. This superb collection of fourteen 4th- or 5th-century pieces of late Roman silver, thought perhaps to be the lost property of a Roman general, has a particularly murky past which has been mired in controversy over the years. Several countries have laid claim to its ownership, for despite its possession by a consortium of 'establishment' art figures and later Spencer Compton, the Marquess of Northampton, the provenance of the treasure has always been somewhat disputed.

Yugoslavia, Lebanon and Hungary have all proffered reasons for their legitimate ownership of the hoard – once valued at £50 million – and its 'hot potato status' has seen subsequent deals and potential sale at auction fall through due to court rulings and 'paperwork irregularities'. The Marquess, despite the many problems, has legally retained ownership and did even exhibit the hoard at Bonhams in 2006. In the latest episode of the saga, the Hungarian government has purchased seven pieces of the treasure for €15 million. Over the years, Hungary's claims as the original source seem to have gathered momentum. It is even claimed that the hoard was found by a young soldier called József Sümegh in the mid-1970s. He was unfortunately found dead in 1980 and the circumstances have not been resolved. It's also thought that there may be other elements of the treasure which have not yet come to light – mainly because there are no smaller artefacts as would commonly be found in such a majestic hoard.

It remains to be seen what will happen to the other seven pieces.

Legless

One of my colleagues on the *Antiques Roadshow* – Philip Taubenheim – runs a particularly good old-school saleroom called Wotton Auction Rooms. I was quite amused by an anecdote about a slightly unusual Black Forest carving of a dog and puppies which appeared in one of his sales. In his usual humorous manner, he described it as being 'in superb condition apart from two legs being missing'. Apparently found in the back of a garage it made a mighty £5,200 – despite the damage!

Favourite Finds

Collecting is not something that you can compartmentalise into an annual activity. Sure enough, there are annual fairs and events that you might look forward to, but collecting is often happenstance; half an hour ago I walked out of my back gate to go and buy a birthday card, now I am the proud owner of a very lovely 19th-century military mahogany chest. Granted, it cost me far more than the £2.79 card but I couldn't resist it as I passed the window of my local antiques shop ... but the *Almanac* wouldn't be the same if I didn't at least pop a few of my favourite personal purchases into its calendrical pages. *So*, here they are:

1. A 17th-century reliquary cabinet or perhaps sacristy cabinet with putto caryatids – full of woodworm and fabulously decorative. Gorgeous!
2. Perhaps one of the best indigenous Japanese models of a house I have ever seen. Made in the late 19th century and comprising a number of separate rooms within a 'courtyard' setting, it surpasses the one in the Victoria & Albert Museum.
3. A wonderful 19th-century French folk art diorama of the grotto at Lourdes, contained in a glass and mahogany case, once owned by me for a short while and prised out of my hands by another collector, only to resurface

at auction where I bought it back – I'd always regretted selling it!

4. A superb early 19th-century Grand Tour vase in the Greek taste, possibly Wedgwood but still undergoing research. Formerly part of a stately collection.

5. A 1950s Hofner Senator 'brunette' (the make, model and colour, respectively) guitar. Another one for the collection …

6. Two wooden foundry dies in the form of large 'cogs', handmade for the purpose of sand-casting pieces for late 19th-century weaving machines. Industrial craftsmanship at its best!

A late 19th-century wooden casting die.

Poles Apart II

In the last edition of the *Almanac*, under the heading 'Poles Apart', I wrote about the amazing discovery of HMS *Erebus*, one of the ill-fated ships on Sir John Franklin's tragic 1845–48 attempt to find the North West Passage. The other ship on the expedition, HMS *Terror*, has still to be found; but the Arctic Medal posthumously awarded to Lt John Irving, the third officer on the *Terror*, recently came to light. The medal was awarded by Queen Victoria in 1857 to 'all persons of every rank and class who have been engaged in the several expeditions to the Arctic Regions ... between the years 1818 and 1855'. This amounted to 1,486 medals in total, the majority of which went to recipients in the Royal Navy.

Irving's story though, is somewhat different to that of his many colleagues who were never seen again and whose mortal remains were never recovered. In 1879, an American search party commanded by Lt Frederick Schwatka made the longest sledge journey then recorded, at over 2,700 miles, in the hope of finding some rumoured papers belonging to the expedition. They found no papers but they did find the remains of Lt John Irving. Among some other graves in a place now known as Camp Crozier, he alone was identified by the presence, next to the skeleton, of a medal which was engraved 'Second mathematical Prize, Royal

Naval College. Awarded to John Irving Mid-summer. 1830'. Irving's remains were subsequently returned to Edinburgh where he was interred in Dean's Cemetery with a fitting memorial. The historic Arctic Medal, from a descendant, was offered by Christie's with an estimate of £20,000–30,000 and realised £37,500.

Black Basalt

Perhaps one of the best pieces of news this year is the announcement that the Wedgwood Museum Collection has been saved for the nation. The museum, due to an error of monumental proportions, became liable for the pottery firm's pension bill after Waterford Wedgwood plc collapsed in 2009. It faced certain disbandment and sell-off unless a large amount of money was raised to save it.

The Wedgwood brand is synonymous with the story of British ceramics. Its history is globally important and its place in the story of industrial innovation, social influence and design cannot be overstated. The loss of such a collection would have been catastrophic for the country. My own passion for Wedgwood extends to several major pieces including a black basalt vase copied from William

Hamilton's collection in the British Museum. It is one of my most treasured objects.

The £15.75 million required was raised in record time. £13 million was injected by the Heritage Lottery Fund and the Art Fund, the balance by public appeal, thus ensuring its continued availability to the general public. The collection is to be gifted to the Victoria & Albert Museum which in turn will re-loan it to the Wedgwood Museum in a new visitor centre at Barlaston.

Butt Man

I have several sporting guns. To be honest, I don't really go shooting much; in fact I find the technical aspects and crafts-manship of my collection far more fascinating than actually letting them off. Mostly, I just clean them – very meticulously. The main problem is that with any paraphernalia-oriented sport, there are so many associated objects for the keen collector to amass. True, it's fun, but it can be expensive too! In reality, I have far too many antique cartridge belts, bags, gun cases and tools; once I'm accessorised for a shoot, I must look rather like a trussed-up chicken. I also shoot black powder but I'll spare you the muzzle-loading wish list on this occasion.

One little rarity that I *don't* have in my collection is something called a 'butt selector'. I know what you are thinking but this is not some sexist device for selecting good-looking bottoms. They look like Vesta cases, usually made of silver, and are in fact produced for a dual purpose: firstly they hold matches; but secondly, they also contain a set of numbered markers which are used to allocate the positions on a driven shoot – very redolent of those sepia-coloured country house weekends with chaps in plus fours toting shotguns! Collectors of 'small silver' particularly like them, as do serious game shooters. A good 1907 example made by the London maker J.C. Vickery was offered by the Nantwich auctioneers Peter Wilson. It had the extra added attraction of a weatherproof match compartment and made an explosive £3,300!

Royal Mug

Royal commemoratives are part of modern life. Tea towels, mugs, keyrings, figurines, medallions and stamps; every coronation, wedding or new royal baby, we expect to be bombarded with a variety of – dare I say it – tasteless 'collectables' that are unlikely, in our own lifetimes, to appreciate much in value. Forgive my cynicism but I've seen rather a lot over the years. However, there are some real commemorative gems around and I would be lying if I didn't admit to having one or two antique ceramic pieces in the house.

Up until the Victorian period, the production of ceramic royal commemoratives had been fairly limited. During the Industrial Revolution, the 'modernisation' of manufacturing techniques and the advent of transfer-printed ceramics started to change that position, although the mass-production of such items was again fairly limited until the advent of the railways and decent roads. Prior to that, the shipping of large quantities of goods and materials over long distances was hard work and mainly carried out on canals and waterways. The potteries did indeed take great advantage of the canal revolution for shipping raw materials and finished products, but it was the Victorian era that saw the greatest expansion.

For aficionados of early royal commemoratives there are a few 'must have' items. Of course, at the top of the tree are the rare 17th-century blue-dash royal portrait chargers of Charles II, which might comfortably set you back £100,000. But for those with a slightly smaller bank balance, a rare 1837 Victoria 'proclamation mug' – a little more difficult to find than a similar-looking Swansea Queen Victoria Coronation mug – might easily cost you £1,000. Some of my favourites are the early creamware pieces, and one of the 'holy grail' mugs among collectors is the very scarce George IV succession mug. The printed black inscription surrounding a portrait of the monarch reads:

God Save The King
Crowned July 19th 1821
George IV Born August 12th 1762
Succeeded To The Throne January 29th 1819.

Interestingly, the date is incorrect: he succeeded to the throne in 1820, and it's often these little idiosyncrasies that ultimately help to bolster the appeal to collectors. Hanson's were lucky enough to offer one as part of a collection of commemorative wares, complete with the usual nibbles, small hairlines and crazing (you will likely never find a really perfect one) and it quickly jumped to a right royal £1,200. A mite more expensive than the latest Will & Kate royal baby mug!

Piano Lesson

Like many youngsters, I was sent to piano lessons. Far from being a chore, it turned out to be quite good fun and one of the real incentives for going each week was that my teacher, Mrs Cook, rewarded my hard work with American comics. Her son had departed the nest some years earlier and had left behind piles of 1960s 'Silver Age' publications. No doubt, in retrospect, there must have been some real gems there, but to me they were simply a veritable treasure trove of fantasy adventure. One of my overriding memories of the comics were the advertisements. As a ten-year-old, I marvelled over the Daisy BB guns, Sea Monkeys (water fleas illustrated as scantily clad anthropomorphic creatures), X-ray spectacles, carbide cannons, hypno-coins and the 200-piece Second World War 'armies' set with its own footlocker for just $1.98! Of course, I now understand that the 'advertising standards authority' was rather lax in those days and the promise of being able to look through a lady's negligee with 'no electricity or batteries required' for just $1 was a baseless con – it seemed pretty good to me, although even then, the prices were slightly out of date and I had no idea how much a dollar was worth.

I paid less attention to the body-building adverts; and for that matter I probably also paid less attention to the technical idiosyncrasies of the artwork than many serious aficionados of the comic medium. However, there are many areas of the comic book genre where both the detail of the art and its underlying meanings have an equally important following. The suggestive artwork and sexuality of characters has long been a controversial topic. One such 'superheroine' is the Phantom Lady, AKA Sandra Knight. She first appeared in 1941 in *Police Comics* (#1). Her subsequent adventures are a little bit more complicated to map but it's her depiction by Matt Baker that is most popular among serious collectors – particularly issue 17 of *Phantom Lady*. The cover, with a hypersexualised image of a scantily clad, buxom heroine bound in ropes, was cited as being morally corruptive to children – to be frank, I don't remember any of the comics from my piano teacher being quite so overt. This form of art is known as 'Good Girl Art' (GGA) and typically emphasises the female attributes in provocative pin-up poses.

Famously, the Phantom Lady was featured as a prime example of the comic genre's negative effect on youth and a major cause of delinquency, in *Seduction of the Innocent*, Fredric Wertham MD's 1954 study. Apparently, it was very widely read and became popular among an older readership – most probably because they too found the many illustrations and moralistic implications of the comic art that they had grown up on quite interesting! Wertham's book led to the formation of the voluntary Comic Codes Authority, which was a self-censoring organisation; however, his work was largely later discredited due to poor sampling, overstated anecdotal assertions and lack of scientific credibility. (He also stated that Wonder Woman was a lesbian – because she was 'independent and strong'!)

A copy of the famous issue was recently sold by Comic Book Auctions in London. It made a bra-busting £1,700!

❧❀❧

Burlesque Beauties

Many years ago I purchased a wonderful 1930s album of saucy watercolours. The subjects, mostly surprised-looking young ladies with fingers innocently touched to their lips, were an amusing assortment of period humour, keyhole voyeurism and French maid fantasies, all executed in that wonderful long-legged, lithe Deco style. I sold a few but still have some; like many other things languishing in folders, I've never quite got around to framing them up.

Naturally such things have a certain appeal to collectors and the appearance of a lot at John Nicholson's in Fernhurst, West Sussex would have been sure to raise a few eyebrows. The lot was comprised of two albums profusely populated with risqué watercolour costume designs by the likes of Virginia Dawn, Michael Bronze, Percival Murray, Ronald Cobb and Hilda Wetton. They were mostly thought to date from the 1940s and 50s; I could easily have envisaged some emblazoned on the nose cone of a Second World War B-17 bomber. However, the origins of these particular designs were somewhat different as they had originally been used for the costumes of the cabaret girls at the infamous Murray's Cabaret Club in Soho.

Opened in 1933, Murray's soon gained notoriety as one of the first topless clubs. It became an infamous celebrity hide-out for royals, gangsters and film stars. The Krays were said to frequent the club, as was Princess Margaret – as an escape from the press. However, the club became even more infamous for its associations with the Profumo affair in which the Conservative Government Minister for War and a Russian spy called Yevgeny Ivanov became embroiled in a scandalous love triangle with Christine Keeler, who was apparently 'managed' by Stephen Ward, the club's 'resident pimp'. Coincidentally, the V&A holds a good number of Ronald Cobb's costume designs, describing him as 'something of a specialist in witty designs for show-girls' costumes'. I tend to agree! The collection sold for £3,800.

Toy Town

The Swiss city of Zürich is famous for many things but one particularly sad recent loss was the wonderful private Spielzeugmuseum (toy museum) of Claudia and Christian

Depuoz. Over several decades they had amassed a superlative collection of rare toys and games with the hope of eventually donating it to the nearby town of Stein am Rhein. Sadly, an agreement could not be reached and what many considered one of the best private collections in Europe, possibly the world, was consigned to the specialist auctioneers Ladenburger Spielzeugauktion. Given the quality and rarity of many lots the competition to acquire some objects was intense; among the collection were two amazing tinplate models: one a Zeppelin in its hangar, made by the company of Georg Heyde, which sold for an astonishing £53,600; and an amazing tinplate townscape dating from around 1880, which at over half a metre high featured a castle on a hill over the town and watermill. It was made by Rock & Graner of Biberach, one of the oldest known commercial toy manufacturers. They went out of business in 1904. It made a very significant £32,400.

❦

Margin Scheme

Margins can be tight in any business. We live in a competitive world and the auction market is just the same. A criticism that's often been levelled at me in my capacity as a valuer is the cost of selling at auction. Commissions vary across different salerooms but what is certain is that they have steadily increased over the years and it's now not uncommon to pay 20–25 per cent when you sell. On top of this charge there can be various extras including insurance, lotting charges, photographic charges, carriage charges and then VAT on all of the peripherals. In some instances, when the goods are being sold by a VAT-registered business, the VAT can also be charged on the hammer price. To add to this, nearly all auctioneers take a commission from the buyer too. It's not always cut and dried because auctioneers often do deals with vendors to entice them into selling collections or good objects; there are also sliding scales involved. Having said that, many people feel quite justified in moaning about the money that auctioneers take and a recent 'inventive' money-making initiative by Christie's met with a plethora of criticism when they announced that they would be charging vendors an extra 2 per cent on lots that exceeded their high estimate. I must admit that I was staggered by such a move. Not only is estimating lots at auction far from being a science, many have argued that, contrary to Christie's argument that 'the purpose is to incentivise', the practice would in fact spawn a culture of undervaluing items expressly to make more money. Auctioneers are often accused of lazy valuing in this respect in any case, but I'm not so sure that this would be the result of the new charge.

However, the media storm within the antiques trade was certainly not a positive result for Christie's PR department and it remains to be seen how vendors feel about such a strangely unquantifiable 'tax on success'.

Yet, despite all these costs, there are many that argue the case for auction as being the most transparent way of buying and selling. Every auction house counter has a leaflet or set of terms and conditions that clearly outline the charges, as opposed to dealers who give no indication of what they paid for an item and how much profit they are making on it. To be honest, things have changed over the decades. There was a time when auctions were strictly the preserve of the trade so in many respects they had the best of both worlds; they endeavoured to control the levels of the wholesale market and then retailed at whatever they thought was the price ... or is that the value? The two are often confused.

These days, the trade rings that used to sew up auction houses (and believe you me I had first-hand experience of the problem) are largely things of the past and auctions are frequented by all sections of society. So, given that auction houses quite publicly advertise their charges, how would the trade feel about publishing their purchase prices, less any costs such as rates, restoration, fuel etc., when selling to members of the public? I have a feeling that this would not wash. At the end of the day an item is worth what someone is willing to pay for it and whatever way you purchase it you generally accept those circumstances, given that they are taking place within the law and within the spirit of common decency. After all, it's not illegal for a supermarket to add whatever it likes on top of its wholesale purchase price; it's just that baked beans don't quite fall into the same category as Rembrandts!

Two's Company

Depictions of Westerners in Eastern art are particularly collectable. I have a passion for images of 18th-century European figures on Chinese export ceramics. I adore the strange idiosyncrasies of styles and customs rendered by undoubtedly skilled painters who were nonetheless completely unfamiliar with the subject – indeed a certain amount of artistic licence must have been deemed acceptable, considering they might just as well have been painting Martians! Many were of course taken from engravings and illustrations supplied by European middlemen. Special orders for personalised dinner services are dotted with myths (perhaps a few tales are true) about the colouring instructions on commissions being physically transferred to the finished design – a hazard, I suppose, of the language barrier! However, the difference between an ordinary 18th-century Chinese famille rose punchbowl and one painted with a Montgolfier hot air balloon can run into the tens of thousands.

In the 18th and 19th centuries the trade with India spawned a whole new genre of art known as 'Company School'. The name derives from India's connection with the British East India Company and the desire of the company officials to take home painted representations of their stay and experiences in this exotic land. For Indian artists it was a new style, a departure from the traditional forms of painting that they were used to under their declining indigenous patronage and a clever amalgamation with the Western desire for accurate perspectives and representation. The use of Western materials also became more widespread and watercolour became a more popular medium, quickly spreading from its origins in the Madras Presidency (an administrative area of British India). Originally founded in 1639, and known as the Agency of Fort St George, the village of Madraspattinam was purchased by the English East India Company as a centre for manufacture and trade. It quickly expanded from the locality and the artistic Anglo-Indian hybrid style of 'Company School' flourished into a generic style of tourist art depicting architecture, dance, portraits of indigenous rulers, landscapes, hunting scenes and so on.

However, it's the early examples of this genre that most excite the market and Canterbury Auction Galleries were recently in a position to offer two wonderful satirical watercolour examples based on a poem by Sir Charles D'Oyly called *Tom Raw, the Griffin – A Burlesque Poem* ... Published in 1828, it's the fictional account of how a young cadet working for the East India Company – known in contemporary parlance as a 'griffin' or greenhorn – managed (or didn't manage, as the case may be) in such a foreign and alien environment. The original prints are both humorous and informative but these two watercolours were exquisitely executed, if not a little damaged, and an excellent

Tom Raw visits Taylor & Co.'s Emporium, Calcutta (print).

example of the 'Company School' aesthetic. At £200–330, the estimate was never going to be of any real relevance and they were snapped up by the London trade at a much heftier £21,000!

❧❧❧

Feather Boa

I was interested to read, in the run-up to the General Election, that the Conservative party had altered their manifesto on the subject of ivory, jettisoning their previously less draconian stance to propose a total ban on its sale in the UK. It's a difficult argument, particularly in the world of art and antiques, where ivory features in the production of many pieces ranging from Japanese netsuke through to painted miniatures and even the lock escutcheons on furniture. Current legislation in the United States prohibits its sale in most states and there are of course rules set out by CITES (the Convention on International Trade in Endangered Species of Wild Fauna and Flora) to prohibit worldwide the sale and movement of any ivory that was sourced after 1947. However, this is frequently flouted by poachers and smugglers, particularly where the Eastern market is concerned. Few would disagree with the idea of saving elephants. It's a terrible trade that is both cruel and rather pointless. Other species too are affected by the demand for archaic Eastern medicines and raw materials. However, the implications for the art market are significant now that the Conservative government is in power.

It's interesting to consider what effect such legislation can have on auction results. As far as the American market is concerned, there are a number of things that cannot be imported into the USA, in effect making the commodity technically worthless to American collectors. However, given that the main illegal markets are not Western and generally ignore such legislation, many are prone to ask, who is most affected?

On the subject of conservation, I recently noticed the sale of a quite historic artefact – another one with a connection to the Franklin Expedition, about which I have written both in last year's *Almanac* and elsewhere in this volume. The object in question, known as a 'lei hula', is a necklace made from the bright yellow feathers of the now extinct Hawaiian 'o'o bird (also known as a honeyeater). This proved no potential barrier to American collectors at Semley's Auction in Dorset, as being extinct means it's far too late to worry about it! As for the Franklin connection, the 'lei' had been presented to Lady Jane Franklin, the wife of the ill-fated Sir John Franklin who was lost on the expedition to find the North West Passage. Lady Jane has become famous for her unrelenting tenacity in trying to find any trace of her husband and the two ships that disappeared on the expedition.

Despite her failure to find him, she was certainly not dissuaded from travelling the globe herself. In 1861, she visited the Sandwich Islands, now known as Hawaii. It was there that, along with Sir John Franklin's niece Sophia Cracroft, she met King Kamehameha IV. At a subsequent meeting with Queen Kalama, widow of the previous king, she was presented with the feather necklace. These golden feathers were once a royal preserve and ownership by commoners was strictly forbidden. Apparently, trained bird catchers were able to remove the feathers without harm but with the arrival of Europeans and their firearms, the 'o'o was hunted to extinction.

The piece came with an impeccable written provenance and other supporting items such as two ambrotypes of the King and Queen. These were sold separately for £6,000. Consigned from the estate of the late Miss Frances Woodward, a wartime decoder at Bletchley Park and the biographer of Lady Jane Franklin, the necklace made a record price of £30,000 plus commission. It went to an American collector.

Coffee Shop Curators

How does one measure the success of a museum?
—J. PAUL GETTY

The modern museum experience is very different to the object-based exhibitions of my childhood. In fact, the idea of filling case upon glass case with a myriad of objects has really become a thing of the past. The problem is, that's the sort of museum I like. It seems that these days, modern museum spaces are mainly preoccupied with entertainment and spectacle rather than lots of exhibits. I can see the reason why, because it can get rather tiring wading your way through collections of similar-looking objects with several children in tow. Personally, knowing that any museum collection is likely to be the tip of an enormous object iceberg submerged in the cellars and warehouses of our most revered institutions, it makes me a little bit annoyed when more of the objects are removed to accommodate people's boredom thresholds. Gawping at multimedia displays and following the arrows to the café and gift shop seems to defeat the object of museums – yet I suppose I can see that radical steps have had to be taken to ensure finance and to continue to make Victorian ideals about collecting more attractive to a modern audience.

'What brought this rant on?' I hear you saying, and

yes, it has been brought home to me when I've visited several galleries and museums lately, scooted past the large explanatory 'idiot' boards and by-passed the sparsely populated cinema. I have admittedly had fun with some of the dressing-up boxes, one aspect of modern museums that I do enjoy. So what of the objects? Where have they been going? One interesting article that piqued my interest contained some enlightening comments by specialist maritime auctioneer Charles Miller; he remarked on the apparent lack of interest shown by the National Maritime Museum in a rather fine and previously unknown early 18th-century Admiralty Dockyard (or Navy Board) ship model. His assertion that the auction at which it appeared had four times as many models on view as the museum actually has on exhibition is an interesting one. I can't verify this but I certainly wouldn't be surprised.

The model itself was a unique example which had been in the same family since the early 19th century. In essence, it was a unique opportunity for the museum to acquire a quite significant model for the national collection. Although prices have declined since the heady days of 2003, when a Queen Anne Navy Board model realised £600,000, perhaps the time might have been right to buy this example for a very reasonable £60,000 – which is what it sold for. Charles Miller's comment that such models are 'generally only seen perhaps once a decade' will add to the scrutiny regarding this apparent malaise. Yet we also all know that museums do not have bottomless budgets, especially during these hard times. However, I'm personally for bringing a few more things out of storage and trying to redress the balance a little; could the general move towards acres of large-scale graphics be tempered by the use of more fascinating objects? After all, that's what we go to museums for – isn't it?

❧❧❧

Irish Times

There's a great fringe benefit to being a writer – travel. As part of the 'post-production/promotional' process of writing *Allum's Antiques Almanac*, I have a very interesting time visiting literary festivals, doing talks for various groups, attending seminars and meeting a number of lovely bookshop owners who selflessly give over their shops for me to chat with their loyal customers and hopefully sign a few of my books. On one such recent expedition I found myself on the stormy coast of the Republic of Ireland in West Cork, a rugged and beautiful place characterised by its complicated coastline, colourful buildings and ancient history. Eager to soak up as much as possible in my short stay (it's often a brief visit when you are on a signing) I was keen to sample the prehistory of the area, the solemnity of Ireland's chequered past and the hospitality of its friendly inhabitants. To this end my whistle-stop tour eagerly took in stone circles, the emotive site of the famine pit in Abbeystrowry cemetery near Skibbereen, where some 10,000 bodies from the great potato famine of 1845–52 are buried in a mass grave (one of many), and several pints of Guinness and Murphy's in a selection of welcoming time-warp bars. Added to this, my evening at Whyte's Books in Schull was a charming mix of locals and visitors, people from the heart of the community who came together to chat and drink wine over the subject that enthrals me most – antiques.

So it was interesting to see for myself the nature of the trade in Ireland, albeit briefly. As a youngster, cutting my teeth in the auction business put me in touch with many Irish buyers – always strong, both in character and spending power. It was way before the days of money-laundering laws, and huge rolls of banknotes would emerge from their baggy pockets to pay for good period pieces of furniture. These hardened, often illiterate buyers were, in their own words, schooled in the 'University of Life' and no messing – they were as sharp as nails. Eighteenth-century Irish furniture, so distinct in style with its carved aprons, scallop shells and grotesque masks, would be the jewel of any auction and I always lit up if I was lucky enough to find any on a general house valuation.

Given the impact of the recession and the demise of the Celtic Tiger, you would think that the last six years or so would have seen a major drop in demand for good Irish antiques but that doesn't seem to have been the case. As the green shoots of recovery tentatively seem to be sprouting on the Emerald Isle, lack of supply seems to be the main problem, rather than an intransigent market. Dublin auctioneers Adam's are well versed in this area and their 'Country House Collections' sales are a popular attraction. Like the British market, buyers are choosey: 'brown' furniture is still difficult; but when special objects come up for sale the competition is always fierce. One recent item of furniture that definitely stood out was an incredibly ornate teapoy, a sort of tea caddy on a stand. This one, carved from bog yew, had been made by one of Dublin's foremost cabinet makers, Arthur Jones & Co., for the 1851 Great Exhibition. Apparently, the company, under the directorship of John Lambert Jones, offered very little for sale at the exhibition, preferring to publicise their skills and raffle the items off later. For the teapoy, 2,000 tickets were sold at a guinea each, a huge amount of money at the time. This furniture maker's tour de force came with a period letter confirming this. It sold for £11,770 – enough money, you might think, but nowhere near as much as the original 2,000 guineas, which translates to over £200,000 pounds in modern money!

Braveheart

Mention the name Robert the Bruce and it's hard not to think of Mel Gibson's epic film *Braveheart*. Although the film centres on Gibson's character, William Wallace (and you are required to suspend your disbelief as far as some of the historical details are portrayed), the figure who is really most central to the film is Robert the Bruce, played by Angus Macfadyen. As the nobleman next in line to the Scottish throne, the film is essentially about his dilemma to follow through Wallace's heroic legacy, with Wallace essentially providing the impetus for Bruce's larger role in history.

As King of Scotland between 1306 and 1329, Robert the Bruce is naturally a figure of great historical importance and a national hero to the Scots. Objects associated with him are scarce and, being half Scottish myself – on my mother's side – I tend to take a keener interest in Scottish matters than I might otherwise do. One such item recently appeared at Timeline Auctions, London, in the form of a 'cokete' seal, which in this case was a two-part seal contained in a later wooden case, used by customs officials at the time of Robert's reign. This particular, well-documented example, known as the Cokete seal of Dunfermline Abbey, dating from 1322 and bearing the legend +ROBERTVS DEI GRACIA REX SCOTORVM (that is, 'Robert, by the Grace of God, King of the Scots'), would normally have been destroyed when obsolete or damaged, but despite some slight fracturing which was most likely caused by use, it had by some quirk of fate survived. Its 19th-century oak box adorned with labels and inscriptions citing its provenance, together with supporting literature, historical notes and context, made this an exciting medieval survivor. Estimated at £80,000–120,000, it was always going to be very difficult to estimate an item like this; as it turned out, it wasn't a bad attempt and the seal matrix topped its higher estimate to make a commission-inclusive £151,250. *Alba gu bràth!*

Bicorn or Tricorn

Cock your hat – angles are attitudes
—Frank Sinatra

I'm a tricorn (or tricorne) man myself. If you have no idea what I'm talking about, it's a style of hat, much beloved of the BBC's new heart-throb Aiden Turner, aka Poldark – and, at the other end of the scale, Chelsea pensioners! Popular in the 18th century, the style apparently developed from the propensity of Spanish soldiers in the 17th century

Napoleon in characteristic bicorn hat.

to fold up the brims of their wide hats into a distinctive triangular shape. The military, aristocrats and commoners alike all adopted this type of hat and it was made in a variety of materials ranging from wool felt to beaver hair felt. They were often embellished with bullion braiding. The bicorn (or bicorne), on the other hand, is a two-cornered later evolution, that also comes in different styles – worn sideways or pointing forwards – and was much favoured by naval and military types. Perhaps the most famous wearer of this style of hat was Napoleon Bonaparte.

So, how many hats did Napoleon have? Estimates seem to hover around 120, used throughout his turbulent tenure of the Empire, but no one can be absolutely sure. There are thought to be nineteen left. Which reminds me about a chap I once knew who I was sure was a Russian spy. One day, as we drank vodka together, he told me an amusing story about a visit by President Mitterand to the USSR. Thinking it would be a nice gesture, it was decided to return one of Napoleon's hats that was languishing in the Russian state archive, as a kind of diplomatic entente cordiale. However, the man with keys (who didn't want to give it away) decided to make himself absent and the surprise handover never took place. I'm not quite sure how true this tale is, but I've had some mileage out of it over the years – suitably embellished, of course.

The recent appearance of one of these surviving iconic pieces of millinery history was at the dispersal of part of the collection of Prince Rainier of Monaco. Largely assembled by Prince Louis II (1870–1949) the collection was displayed as a museum by Rainier. The hat, complete with original silk lining, had a provenance dating back to a veterinarian of the Imperial Household, Joseph Giraud. Media attention was unprecedented and the hammer finally fell to a Mr T.K. Lee, a representative of Harim Group's billionaire owner, the South Korean food company mogul Kim Hong-Kuk. Odd, you might think – me too – but apparently he regards Napoleon's influence as a 'guiding spirit for modern entrepreneurs'. The hat cost him almost £1.5 million pounds, including commission.

Sunny Side Up

What's the most expensive egg in the world? Most people would probably think that it was a trick question and go for the Fabergé option, but in this instance I'm more interested in real eggs. Nor am I talking about rogue collectors who might pay high prices to illegally acquire rare bird's eggs – under the 1981 Wildlife and Countryside Act it is illegal to offer wild birds' eggs for sale. However, the eggs of the now extinct Elephant bird from Madagascar are certainly not illegal to sell.

Elephant birds come from the family Aepyornithidae, and are one of several varieties of once-prolific very large flightless birds. Their nearest living relative is the Kiwi. Despite historical accounts of the birds, the reasons for their extinction are somewhat unexplained, although man is most likely the cause. No reports of them exist after the late 17th century, yet there is plenty of evidence of their existence in both the fossil and sub-fossil records, and particularly in the large amounts of eggshell that still litter their original habitats. The eggs, up to 160 times the size of a chicken's egg, are greatly prized by collectors and museums, despite all the shell fragments that survive, because very few are intact. There are thought to be only around 60 complete examples in existence.

The word sub-fossil describes something that is not

fossilised, or only partly fossilised, and in the case of organic items, DNA can be extracted from extremely old specimens. In the case of Elephant bird eggs, unbroken examples can contain complete, immature birds. In 2013 an intact egg with a skeleton inside was sold by Christie's for over £66,000 (including commission). More recently another example, complete with a CT scan attesting to its structural integrity, was sold by Summers Place Auctions for a slightly lighter premium-exclusive £54,000. Its new home is in China.

Record Breaker

I was slightly amused to see an advert in the trade press for an inaugural collector's sale at an auction house. Mentioned and illustrated as a 'highlight', was an HMV No. 109 table-top phonograph, a typical oak-cased example dating from the late 1920s. Described by many connoisseurs of such machines as the stalwart record player of the period, the 109 was based on a model dating from around 1913 and in reality had changed very little from its predecessors. In fact, they were so rock-solid and reliable that people were quite happily and routinely using them to play their 78s well into the 1960s – and I'm sure some people still do. The 109 cost around £10 10s in 1929 – a considerable amount of money – yet, after all these years, they are only worth around £50–100 at auction. Still, they can be quite good fun if you want something on which to play your collection of Caruso.

Note, these are not to be confused with the Columbia model 109 dating from around the same period – a commonly available portable in a rexine-covered hinged case – which in modern terms is far from portable but is again a good, reliable player. Similarly, they sell for around £50–80 at auction and, like the HMV No. 109, are generally not regarded as a major sale highlight!

Mud Bath

The aim of art is to represent not the outward
appearance of things, but their inward significance.
—Aristotle

It's a subject that splits opinion down the middle – *is it art?* Contemporary 'Land Artist' Richard Long is the sort of person that divides opinion. Famous for his monumental works within landscapes, I personally love the scale of his installations and the effortless symbiotic relationship that his sculpture has in its relationship with the natural and man-made surroundings in which he places it. For me, it echoes the ancient Nazca correlation that their geoglyphs have in the deserts of southern Peru. He is the only artist to have been nominated four times for the Turner Prize.

Among his works are what some might consider 'controversial' mud 'drawings', consisting of paper dipped in mud from the River Avon in Bristol and either left to dry or worked manually with hands or feet. Inevitably, some are moved to ask, 'Is this art?' Whatever your opinion, as a master of conceptual art, he makes work that is both popular and valuable. Often displayed in multiples, an example of his worked mud was entered for sale at Mallams Auctioneers. Apparently, it had been exhibited some fifteen years ago, as part of a bigger work, at the Royal West of England Academy, Bristol. It came with a letter which authenticated its provenance. The swirls of mud applied by hand could, on the face of it, be the daubs of a child, but herein lies the contextual conundrum of modern art, for like my attempt in last year's *Almanac* to create a 'Rothko', no child could emulate the presence in Long's work, and despite it being an incomplete piece, it sold for £3,800.

Scrap Heap

Many years ago, while working in the London auction business, I was rather interested to see that we had taken delivery of what looked like a pile of scrap bronze. The long sectional pieces obviously went together to form a sculpture and on further inspection it also turned out to be signed – 'Isamu Noguchi'. The consignment note said, 'pieces of metal', or words to that effect.

Noguchi was a highly influential Japanese-American designer, architect and artist. Born in 1904, he was the son of the highly acclaimed Japanese poet Yone Noguchi and the writer Léonie Gilmour. His post-war career saw him working for the Herman Miller Company in collaboration with other design luminaries such as Charles Eames and George Nelson. Their subsequent body of work is considered by many to be among the most influential catalogues of modern design in the 20th century. Herman Miller still produces the iconic Noguchi table, a masterful blend of simplistic sculptural brilliance applied to a practical form.

Unsurprisingly, Noguchi's work attracts significant attention when it comes up for sale and one such piece, another early and unique example of sculptural furniture – also a table – was sold by Phillips in their 'Icons of Design' auction in New York. Made in 1939 for Anson Conger Goodyear, the noted philanthropist and patron of the arts who was the first president of the Museum of Modern Art, the table, which subsequently passed through several hands, had originally been in Goodyear's home in Nassau County, a stunning modernist building designed by architect Edward Durell Stone in the International style and finished in 1938. The building is now listed in America's National Register of Historic Places. A good pedigree, I'm sure you'll agree. The table sold for £2.6 million!

However, the 'pile of scrap' turned out to be one of an edition of six bronze sculptures entitled *Mortality* and dated 1961. It was rather begrudgingly returned to the right place with a 'do you know what this is?' note attached to it and was eventually sold for $433,600. It would have looked lovely in the garden!

※彩ぐ⁂

Churchill's Crown

Without tradition, art is a flock
of sheep without a shepherd
—WINSTON CHURCHILL

2015 is the 50th anniversary of the death of one of Britain's greatest statesmen and wartime leaders – Sir Winston

Churchill. Twice prime minister, in 1940–45 and 1951–55, Churchill's career saw him serve as a soldier and politician while becoming renowned as a great orator, historian and artist, and the man who inspired Britain to resist and eventually defeat the Nazis. This anniversary year has been a good reason for the nation to revisit the life of the man known as one of the most influential people in British history.

Naturally, as well as a number of worldwide commemorative exhibitions, concerts and memorial events, there have been quite a few associated specialist sales and auctions. With respect and reverence to the great man, I've picked a few of the most interesting stories associated with this anniversary.

I was barely a few months old when Churchill died. His state funeral, a fitting honour bestowed upon him by Queen Elizabeth, was the biggest of its type with 112 representatives from countries around the world attending. After lying in state in Westminster Abbey for three days he was conveyed to his final resting place at St Martin's Church in Bladon after the service on a special funeral train pulled by the Battle of Britain class locomotive *Winston Churchill*. My earliest memories of Churchill's legacy were due to the several commemorative crowns (five-shilling pieces) that were kept in our home. Issued after his death, some 19,640,000 were struck – a colossal amount. As a result, they are of little commercial value and I continue to see them on a very regular basis – however, as a mark of respect, they serve as an apt vehicle for that sentiment.

In 2003 I was lucky enough to visit Chartwell in Kent, the home of Winston and his wife Clementine, where we filmed an *Antiques Roadshow*. It was very special to experience the house and be in such close proximity to objects that almost radiated the presence of the great man himself. The house itself was given to the National Trust by Clementine after Churchill's death, a generous gesture made possible by a consortium of businessmen who in 1945 purchased the estate from the Churchills (it was expensive to run) and rented it back to them at a more affordable rate. This was for the duration of their lives, on the proviso that it went to the Trust afterwards. Clementine could have stayed at Chartwell following Winston's death but chose to give it to the Trust straight away.

I suppose, of all the symbols in history that have denoted famous people, the cigar is Winston's iconic epitaph. Apparently, he gained a liking for cigars on a visit to Cuba in 1895, where his thirst for a career-enhancing experience led him into the conflict that erupted when Cuba was rebelling against its Spanish masters. By all accounts, Churchill would stock some 3,000–4,000 cigars in a special room in Chartwell. His favourite brands were Romeo y Julieta and Aroma de Cuba (no longer made). He smoked around eight or ten cigars a day but would often let them go out and chew them instead – as a result they would become much frayed. His cigar-smoking exploits are legendary and the idiosyncrasies of his habit are too numerous to mention here; however, the result of smoking such large amounts means that he left plenty around for the souvenir-hunters – both smoked and unsmoked! They are very collectable and have over the years made a variety of prices. In 2010, a hastily stubbed-out example, unfinished on the day that the advancing German army reached Leningrad, made £4,200! Usually they are a little cheaper but given the frequency with which they tend to occur, they fetch remarkably high amounts.

Churchill at his desk in Downing Street.

Other interesting Churchill artefacts – of the non-smoking variety – also attract attention and in 2011, Keys auctioneers offered a partial set of Winston's false teeth, which sold for over £15,000. However, in this momentous year it has been the sale of the late Mary Soames, Churchill's cigar-smoking youngest daughter that has registered some of the biggest values. She was the fifth and last child of Winston and Clementine. Born in 1922, she grew up at Chartwell, later joining the ATS during the war and then becoming Churchill's aide-de-camp, a highly responsible position that put her in close contact with leading wartime figures such as Stalin and Roosevelt. The sale of items from her estate, by Sotheby's, was bound to cause interest and the £12.8 million total was indicative of the many personal and historically connected items that were put under the hammer. A painting by Churchill, *The Goldfish Pool*, sold for a record-breaking £1.5 million. A silver water jug by Comyns and Sons, given to Churchill on his birthday by a member of the War Cabinet and inscribed 'Egypt 1942' – referring to the battle of El Alamein – took £230,000 on a £4,000–6,000 estimate! One extremely poignant little item was a silver matchbox sleeve which had been given to Churchill as a Christmas present from his children. The inscription reads:

PAPA, WITH LOVE FROM DIANA, RANDOLPH,
SARAH, MARY, CHRISTMAS, 1927.

It was estimated at £300–500 but realised a staggering £55,000. These are just a few lots from an historic sale. No doubt there will be many other associated items finding their way to market before the end of the year.

⁂

American Beauty

Some twelve years ago, in North Wales, I filmed a very interesting piece about a local man who lived a rather eccentric double life as a professional supplier of firewood and a proxy Native American. He not only dressed the part but also lived in a tepee – weather permitting. Sadly, he had passed away, but his collection had been inherited by a lady who wanted to know how best to deal with it. Among his possessions were a number of publications by Grey Owl, aka Archibald Belaney; born in Hastings in 1888, Belaney adopted an identity as an Ojibwa Indian and in the early 20th century became well known as an early conservationist and environmentalist. After his death, his reputation was tarnished by the revelation that he was British-born. Some accused him of being a fake, although his work and reputation have latterly been rehabilitated and recognised. Richard Attenborough directed the 1999 biopic 'Grey Owl' starring Pierce Brosnan. The Welsh story certainly reflected Belaney's past and was quite moving, especially when the lady announced that she was looking after the gentleman's horse, which had pulled his wood cart and doubled as his native steed!

Among his possessions were some headdresses fashioned from eagle feathers. The sale of such feathers is prohibited by law in America under the act which protects both bald eagles and golden eagles. Eagle feathers are traditionally much prized by Native Americans and the birds are much revered in religious and symbolic terms. Native American acquisition of feathers is permitted within the limits of relevant permits – mainly for religious purposes – but is strictly controlled. When I filmed my piece, several of the items were affected by this protective legislation and could not be sold in the USA.

Considering the effect of this legislation on the move-ment of such material, I was interested to see whether this would affect the fate of a rare Native American outfit that was coming up for sale with Fonsie Mealy Auctioneers of County Kilkenny in Ireland. The mountain sheep-hide construction of the poncho, war shirt and leggings reflected that of plains Indians such as the Lakota Sioux and Cheyenne, with painted decoration and porcupine quillwork. It also had an eagle feather bonnet. The outfit came with a long provenance dating from the 1860s and heralded from the distinguished family of the late Jane Avril de Montmorency Wright. In fact, the issue of the feathers made no difference whatsoever, with a number of American buyers attending both the saleroom and bidding online and on the telephone. The outfit quickly surpassed its €4,000–6,000 estimate to make €320,000 – to an American private buyer. I can only assume that he would have left the headdress behind to find another market perhaps? A slight shame – after all this time it seems sad they couldn't be kept together, but that's the law.

※⁂⁂⁂※

Budgie Smuggler

Smoking. We know the facts. It's plainly very harmful to your health, but since the 17th century when we started smoking the 'evil weed', the ritual of lighting up, chewing tobacco or taking snuff has created a vast swathe of collectable paraphernalia. Commonly known in collector's circles as 'tobacciana', it ranges from tobacco boxes to cigarette holders, vesta cases, lighters, pipe tampers, cigarette cards and cigar cutters, to name but a few. Lighters, particularly, occupy a strong niche in the market and Dunhill, the famous luxury goods company founded in 1893, were well known for making interesting and innovative lighters, including larger tabletop varieties.

The famous 'Aquarium' lighters of the 1940s and 50s are particularly sought after and can make thousands of pounds. The bodies are made of Perspex panels that are reverse-carved and hand-coloured to give a three-dimensional effect and, like many objects that surpass the purpose of their original intent, they are now regarded as decorative objects. Although many are ornamented with fish – as the name suggests – there are also many other different designs. I like the budgies. They have a slightly kitsch quality but are far from kitsch in price. Bonhams recently sold one in their 'Gentleman's Library' sale for £2,200.

Bear Witness

Themed auctions are nothing new; auctioneers rely on them as a clever form of promotion and as a vehicle for bringing together related material that can, as a result, meet a more dedicated niche market. So no doubt there was some consideration of the publicity possibilities when Sotheby's were able to mount a quite unusual sale entitled 'Bear Witness'. Billed as 'one of the auction house's largest ever sales' the anonymous single-owner collection comprised a superb selection of modern art and sculpture featuring works by Rothko, Giacometti, Warhol and Allen Jones. Also, and hence the title, the sale included a large number of lots of art and antiques related to bears (as well as skulls and memento mori). Prices ranging from just £50 to hundreds of thousands were mooted as being inclusive to all collectors, although I smiled at the estimate on two carved meerschaum opium pipes in a case, which, estimated at £50–70, realised £9,375. However, the lots on offer ranged from children's teddy bear tea sets to superlative modern art. The result: a cool Fox's Glacier Mint bear of a total, at just over £36 million!

Yellow Midget

The art and auction world abounds with tales of missing treasures and rare variations hitherto unseen but rumoured to exist. I remember around 30 years or so ago, people were convinced of the existence of a fabled rare yellow version of the Bakelite camera known as the Coronet Midget. These tiny little cameras, sometimes known as sub-miniature cameras, were made by the Coronet Camera Company of

Birmingham, and were introduced in 1935. Although a novelty rather than a serious camera, their 16mm format could take six images using a fixed focus lens with a fixed shutter speed, and they are popular among collectors. They came in various colours including black, brown, two shades of green, a mottled orange and a mottled red. The rarest, however is the blue, introduced in 1937; in contrast to the fairly plentiful brown, for instance, which is worth £30–50, Golding Young & Mawer of Bourne recently sold a blue version for £290. As for the fabled yellow example? Apparently, it was fake using an enhanced picture that was meant to perhaps fool a camera collector. No one has ever seen a real yellow version.

Weight of the World

'Adriaen de Vries is the Dutch Michelangelo'. These were the words of Wim Pijbes, general director of the Rijksmuseum in Amsterdam on their recent acquisition of a superb metre-high bronze figure of Atlas by the Mannerist master de Vries – Mannerism being a period in European art that evolved from the Italian High Renaissance, which subsequently evolved into the Baroque period in the late 16th century. Mannerist style is characterised by unusual perspectives, highly stylised poses and elongated proportions.

De Vries was born in The Hague in 1556. His career as a draughtsman, sculptor and bronze founder took him across Europe working with contemporaries such as Giambologna. His immense skill wooed the likes of many great art connoisseurs and collectors, including Emperor Rudolph II. The Victoria & Albert Museum has a superb bust of Rudolph made by de Vries at his Prague workshops in 1609 (collection number 6929-1860). As one of the great Mannerist sculptors, his work has often been called 'a well-kept secret' among art historians but an exhibition organised by the Rijksmuseum, the Getty and the National Museum in Stockholm in 1998 at last shone the spotlight on this Dutch master, finally propelling him to greater public appreciation as an artist who capably bridged both the Mannerist and Baroque periods. Although his work is held by several international museums, his own country of origin has always suffered a somewhat unfair dearth of his sculpture.

The appearance at Christie's of a previously unrecorded figure was a good opportunity for this situation to be remedied. Signed *Adrianvs Fries 1626*, the bronze figure of Atlas was found in the centre of an ornamental pool in the courtyard of Schloss Sankt Martin in Austria in 2010.

It had been there since at least 1700, as an engraving of the period recorded it in situ. Despite a previous delay in sale caused by an export licence glitch, the piece was featured as a central attraction in the Christie's 'Exceptional' sale. It was suggested that the Bacchic attributes of the sculpture may have meant its thematic origins were changed partway through the process, to its present form as Atlas. Apparently the alloy in the globe above his head differs slightly from that of the main figure. Interesting! Anyway, the figure caused much interest and was purchased by the Rijksmuseum for a staggering £16.6 million, more than half of the actual sale total.

✳✳✳

Stick Shift

Speak softly and carry a big stick; you will go far
—THEODORE ROOSEVELT

Naïve folk art, scrimshaw and Napoleonic prisoner-of-war art are highly sought after by collectors. I eagerly search out small marine ivory carvings, prisoner-of-war bone oddities and naïvely executed little pictures and portraits. The Americans are particularly fond of collecting such things, and objects fashioned by whalers and sailors from the 18th and 19th centuries can command high prices. Elaborate walking canes are one such area and have a crossover appeal, gaining interest from both cane collectors and folk art aficionados.

The best examples are fashioned from a mixture of whalebone and marine ivory and inlaid with combinations of tortoiseshell and baleen, sometimes silver coins too. Typically, they were made for sale to tourists when in port; the sailors were capable of executing remarkably complicated sectional canes and modern collectors love to see a variety of different designs and disciplines incorporated into the sticks. In 2012, Perry & Phillips of Bridgnorth in Shropshire auctioned off a particularly good one with pictorial whaling scenes, which realised £46,000. In 2013, Bigwood of Teddington sold one for £27,000. The latest example to come to sale didn't quite reach these heights but for a local couple close to Cottees Auctioneers of Wareham, they were amply rewarded when their inherited cane, complete with architectural barley twist sections, made a substantial £11,000.

Masthead

I come across some odd things. The other day I was in a house and spotted a cannonball on the floor in the corner of a room. It turned out to have been dredged from the moat of a castle that had been laid siege in the English Civil War. That's very much the type of thing I like to buy – in fact, I wouldn't mind having my own cannon, but despite having a black powder licence I have refrained from going down that route, making do instead with the spectacle of the re-enactments in my local park, provided by the impressive ordinance of the English Civil War Society (ECWS). It really makes the windows rattle!

Where is this leading, I hear you say? Well, there's a cannonball connection and it's an association with Nelson's famous flagship HMS *Victory* – a ship I've visited several times, a fascinating window back into history, frozen at a point where Britain's naval and military prowess put it first in the world order. The interesting thing about the *Victory* is that, at 250 years old, she has had to undergo several refits and restorations, not least from battle damage sustained during her long and distinguished career. It's not really known how much of the *Victory* dates to Nelson's time, let alone to the date of her launch in 1765. What is certain is that a large percentage of her has been replaced and repaired, and it's thought that as much as 30 per cent of her was already substituted by the time Nelson inherited her. As a result of this, a great number of souvenirs have been fashioned from these leftover pieces. I've owned several objects, such as copper plaques made from the hull sheathing – many were made for the centenary celebrations of the battle of Trafalgar in 1905.

Hansons Auctioneers of Etwall offered something similar in one of their sales: an item made of the wood from the shattered foremast of *Victory* after the damage she sustained at Trafalgar. In fact, the damage was so bad that all her masts had to be replaced after the battle. A piece of the original mast has been preserved on the lower gun deck, and it has a large hole through it, a distance of some 80cm, caused by a single shot, thought to have come from the French ship *Redoutable*. The lot offered by Hansons was a model of the foremast and, at 1.35m high, was a useful commemorative chunk of the ship. Along with the mast was an explanation of all the shot holes caused by the devastating volley fired by the *Redoutable*. *Victory* now sports Victorian iron and wood masts but the construction of these colossal spars was an incredible feat of construction and it's interesting to note the sectional spliced nature of the original, cleverly constructed masts. The model sold for £2,200, which I felt was a little on the cheap side but what a great memento!

Blood is Thicker

History will be kind to me, for I intend to write it.
—WINSTON CHURCHILL

Sometimes, when selling items, it's necessary to exercise some sensitivity. Making that judgement – which I've had to do on several occasions – depends on various factors: major tragedies, loss of life, criminal cases, the Nazis, and dubious macabre circumstances can all be issues; yet the fact is, we humans thrive on such tales, our morbid fascination acting as a catalyst for collecting the weird and the wonderful. So when do things become unfit for sale? Frankly, opinions will always differ. We can't rewrite history and scrub away all that we don't like, however contentious or horrible these events may have been, yet sometimes the fatal attraction of some objects is such that they are best put away, archived for their own safety and for the safety of others. For this reason I will not handle Nazi material; it's a personal preference but one that is not universally shared within the business – there is a strong collecting fraternity for such items.

However, I was not wholly surprised to see that a lot pertaining to Winston Churchill had been withdrawn from sale at the request of the family. At the age of 87, Churchill broke his hip while on holiday in Monte Carlo. He was flown back to London in an RAF jet and treated at the Middlesex Hospital, where blood samples were taken. Churchill was very ill. After he also contracted pneumonia, many thought he might not survive the ordeal. One phial of blood, which was taken by a student nurse called Patricia Fitzgibbon, was never used and she asked if she could keep it. Permission was granted and the glass phial containing the blood of the great man was kept as a keepsake until it surfaced at Duke's of Dorchester, after Patricia's death. I must admit, I personally didn't feel that this was an error of judgement on the auctioneer's part – this was indeed a rare memento of a highly important man – although I suppose it's not too difficult to imagine how the family might feel, knowing that this phial of Churchill's DNA, a very small but meaningful part of him, was about to be sold to a bidder who would be outside of their control. Perhaps there are those that might argue that a lock of hair is no different; was this exploitation at all or rather the opportunity to come as close to this iconic person as it's possible to get? I think perhaps it would have been good to see such a personal piece entrusted to an organisation like the Wellcome Foundation. As for the value? We will never know – the phial has apparently been destroyed.

Arms House

Announcements of startling finds and potential blockbuster lots often appear in the press months before they are sold. Of course, the pre-publicity is always important for heightening the profile of the auction houses and the trade, but it also ensures maximum exposure to the market in order that the piece in question will make the most amount of money possible. The problem for me is that many of these prospective *Allum's Antiques Almanac* stories are frequently dangled like carrots that may or may not make it into my carefully crafted stew of tasty titbits.

The skill is trying to keep track of them, waiting to see what the final result might be or whether the story just disappears into oblivion – which happens more than you might imagine, and for all manner of reasons. Sometimes ownership is called into dispute and lots are withdrawn from sale. Vendors are also known to change their minds, and on other occasions objects are sold by private treaty and withdrawn from sale at the last minute. The most embarrassing situation is when items make large amounts of money, hit the headlines – and are then not paid for. It's a problem auctioneers often face and in recent years it's even become normal practice to take sizeable bidding deposits to try and stop buyers defaulting, particularly those based in foreign countries.

So it's always a little infuriating when you find that a great story that has been on the bubble for a while just sinks without trace. Luckily, I'm a bit of a sleuth and it's usually possible to get to the root of it; sometimes it just requires a quick telephone call so see what has happened and then, if the problem is a little delicate, move on to the next thing.

There was, however, a great little discovery which took a few months to come to fruition. It relates to a chance find when a small cottage in Hanwell was undergoing some restoration work. As the plaster was removed the builders noticed that there were some neatly cut and faced blocks concealed in the wall. When prised out, they were obviously carved verso and as more were revealed it transpired that they were all part of a large stone jigsaw puzzle that formed a high-quality Tudor royal coat of arms – although not quite complete. It's thought the coat of arms probably came from nearby Hanwell Castle, a large mock-fortified house built in the late 15th century by the Cope family, who had links with Henry VIII's last wife Catherine Parr. The castle, now much altered, probably housed the stone armorial above a grand internal fireplace and subsequent alterations saw it recycled locally as building material. Scholars and the press were keen to emphasise the importance of the find but it eventually came up for sale at J.S. Auctions of Banbury, where it sold for £8,000; not a bad little bonus for something that was accidentally discovered entombed in a wall. Whereas I had to wait a few months to round off the story of the discovery, the coat of arms had patiently waited several hundred years!

Black Magic

Some years ago, while sitting at my table on *Antiques Roadshow* duty, I was handed a rather flamboyant-looking walking cane. Set in the top was an ancient Egyptian scarab and I was immediately struck by the powerful aura that seemed to emanate from the cane. Call me superstitious, but my feelings were quickly compounded by the fact that the cane had belonged to the infamous English occultist Aleister Crowley. Born in 1875 and educated at Cambridge University, he was popularly portrayed in the press as a Satanist, although this is not true. At one time he was lambasted as 'the wickedest man in the world' and this was in no small part due to his proclamation that he was a prophet of the religion of Thelema, which he founded, and also his scandalous reputation as a drug user, bisexual and Nazi sympathiser. However, many thought that he was a spy and he himself said that he used his sympathies as cover to infiltrate Nazi groups. Despite all this, his legacy is large

— and complicated. As a poet, novelist and writer of occult literature, Crowley is a significantly influential figure in esoteric counterculture and pop culture circles. I put the cane forward to be filmed but it was thought to be a little contentious. Perhaps that might have been partly due to our position in the schedule after *Songs of Praise*!

Given the interest that Crowley attracted in the press, there are some amazing and quite startling photographs of him; ever the showman, he is often portrayed with glaring eyes and wearing unusual clothing. One such iconic photograph taken in 1934 by the Associated Press shows him in a black-and-white-striped three-piece North African outfit,

The iconic 1934 photo of Aleister Crowley.

complete with a dagger. The clothing, together with the dagger, was apparently subsequently left by Crowley to Deirdre Patricia Maureen Doherty, the mother of his son Aleister Ataturk. It was recently sold by Dreweatts for £11,000, with the dagger being sold separately for £10,000. Crowley died in Hastings in 1947 at the age of 72. I can't help wondering if those items were imbued with the same aura that emanated from the cane.

❧❧❧

Time Team

When I was a boy I decided to create my own time capsule. Time capsules are not a new idea. For centuries, people have seen them as a way of sealing a moment in time for the interest of future generations. Many have been placed as commemorative markers, symbols under memorials, particularly within important buildings and for historic occasions. My version comprised a large glass jar with a screw-on lid in which I placed a strange collection of objects that I thought – from my child's-eye perspective – would interest a future archaeologist who might happen to be digging up the blackcurrant patch in my parents' back garden. I can't exactly remember what I chose but I do remember putting in some coins – an essential object in time capsules – some newspaper clippings and a handwritten note with my name. After some weeks I became bored with the idea of waiting for future generations to retrieve it, and went to dig it up. However, I couldn't find it and, who knows, it may still be there, some forty years later. Unfortunately, the lid will probably have rotted through and no doubt the contents will be in very poor condition!

But it was on the subject of time capsules that I recently saw a fascinating American story about an example that had been sealed in a large quoin (corner stone) of the Massachusetts State House. Apparently, due to some potential water ingress problems, it was decided to extricate the brass box to ensure that its contents weren't under threat. It was clear to see why such care needed to be taken as the time capsule had originally been instigated in 1795 by the then governor of the state, Samuel Adams, along with the famous American silversmith and patriot Paul Revere and associate Colonel William Scollay.

The box, plastered into the bottom of the quoin, was carefully removed, put under police escort and taken to be conserved at the Boston Museum of Fine Arts. X-rays showed that a number of items such as coins, papers and a silver plate made by Paul Revere were present, and when the box was opened it revealed some wonderful treasures: 24 coins in total, and five newspapers. (Some objects had been added in 1855, when the capsule was last opened, again during building renovations.) One of the coins was a rare 1652 'Pine Tree' shilling. This priceless piece of history will no doubt be put back under the State House in a secure container, perhaps with some additional items — as seems customary when reburying time capsules ... I wonder what *I* would put in one now?

❧❦❧

Ring-a-Ding

I grew up on J.R.R. Tolkien's *The Lord of the Rings*. I read it aged eleven; my parents were ardent Hobbit fans and we even had a little cabin cruiser called *Gollum* which used to slither through the waters of the river Avon on balmy summer days — happy memories. Naturally, it was this affiliation that sent me straight off to the cinema at the beginning of Peter Jackson's record-breaking epic trilogy and head over heels into love with a pointy-eared elf maiden called Arwen, played by Liv Tyler! Of course, memorabilia associated with the films is highly collectable but there were an awful lot of props fashioned for the trilogy, which means that in order to achieve really high prices they have to be key objects. Yet when it comes to valuing such things it's almost impossible because it's hard to gauge just how much ardent fans and collectors are prepared to pay. A good example of this was at an auction of movie memorabilia held by Profiles of History in California where the staff used by Gandalf, played by Sir Ian McKellen, was offered for sale. It was estimated at $25,000 but ended up selling for $390,000 (£245,000)! Hard to imagine spending a quarter of a million pounds and standing in front of a mirror pretending to do battle with Saruman!

Out of Time

It drives me insane when I see objects in films and television programmes that are the wrong period. Quite simply, I'm always convinced it's laziness or lack of knowledge on the part of the set and props people – but I suspect that sometimes it's perhaps just too difficult to source the correct items, or risk using period pieces that are too valuable to handle. However, in such cases I also suspect that it's hoped that 99 per cent of people just won't notice. A case in point was the recent production of *Wolf Hall*. Although I did actually really enjoy it, there were a few moments when the props momentarily jarred, particularly when Thomas

Cromwell secreted an object into a Victorian box with a Bramah lock – arrrrgh! The popular remake of *Poldark* had a few problems in the period props department too, and it made me cringe when he sold his father's Victorian watch in the 18th century! Other well-publicised blunders from the series include press photos with a picture of a burglar alarm on a building, along with electrical cables and a television aerial.

Some people make a hobby of spotting such errors and the internet abounds with sites full of filmic faux pas and continuity problems. *Game of Thrones*, which incidentally I also enjoy, while suspending all disbelief, looks like a set decorator's shopping-trolley visit to the prop industry's answer to B&Q, with its curly wrought iron candelabra and patio sets, yet it works well because, being fantasy of a sort, it gets away with it. So when I moan I am usually being a little tongue-in-cheek, and conversely I do love a really good anachronistic science fiction film – call me a steampunk! And now to the point ...

A few years ago, Gergely Barki, a researcher and art historian from the Hungarian National Gallery, was watching the Hollywood film *Stuart Little* with his daughter Lola. In the background of a scene he noticed a painting above a fireplace and realised it was a long-lost work by Hungarian avant-garde artist Róbert Berény (1887–1953). Part of a group known as The Eight, he introduced Expressionism and Cubism to Hungary. Berény had a romance with Marlene Dietrich and was also rumoured to have had an affair with Anastasia, the daughter of Tsar Nicholas II. The picture in the film, *Sleeping Woman with a Black Vase (Woman Asleep)*, had been missing since 1928 and it's thought likely that the original purchaser, who bought the picture from an exhibition that year, may have been Jewish and left Hungary before or during the Second World War. The picture had apparently been purchased by the set designer from an antiques shop in Pasadena for a relatively small amount. After spotting the picture, Barki's flurry of letters eventually paid off and the painting was recently auctioned by the Virág Judit Gallery and Auction House in Budapest where it sold for £179,200. Well spotted Barki!

Cock Up

I'm sometimes a little wary of some of the stories that I hear about or read on the web. One such archaeological nugget worried me slightly, enough for me to check that the date of publication was not 1 April, and to cross-reference it several times with other reliable sources. It's a little rude, so skip this one if you are easily offended.

Archaeologists working in the Polish city of Gdansk were carrying out excavations in a latrine. Among the many objects that were found, including parts of wooden swords – a fact which pointed to it being the site of a fencing school – the excavators were surprised to find a completely intact, leather eight-inch dildo. Dating from the later part of the 18th century, the large phallus was in a remarkable state of preservation due to the anaerobic conditions of the ancient latrine. Fashioned from stitched leather and apparently filled with some form of bristles, it had a naturalistically carved wooden head. Speculation was that it had accidentally been dropped down the toilet by a visitor to the latrine, probably a costly and frustrating accident at the time, as the dildo was almost certainly a pricey custom job. It's currently undergoing preservation.

❦❧❦

Real or No Real

Attribution – it's that old chestnut again. So much can hinge on it that the art world is often sent into flurries of denial and buck-passing as a result of due diligence issues and historic differences on whether pictures are wrong or right. A couple of recent stories revolve around Peter Paul

Rubens (1577–1640), the Flemish Baroque painter, whose sizeable studio in Antwerp produced a large number of pictures for the collectors, nobility and aristocrats of Europe.

Museums sometimes de-accession objects and works of art to reinvest in other items. The Metropolitan Museum of Art in New York did so in 2013 with around sixteen works sent to auction, including a portrait of Rubens' daughter. Prior to the late 1950s it was deemed to truly be by Rubens, but was downgraded to a 'follower of Peter Paul Rubens' by the scholar Julius Held in 1959. One problem was that it had no provenance prior to 1930, but when offered for sale, by Sotheby's, with an estimate of $20,000–30,000, it instantly raised alarm bells by selling for $626,500! This year it was heralded by Ben van Beneden, director of the Rubenshuis in Antwerp as a true portrait by Rubens, possibly of his daughter Clara Serena Rubens. Of course, the inference that the Met had sold off a real Rubens without enough care was picked up in the press. The attribution is still hotly contested by other specialists.

More currently, the latest Rubens to be reattributed was offered by Christie's in their 'Old Master and British Drawings' sale in New York with a catalogue description showing that it had been sold by Phillips in 1999 as 'attributed to Rubens'. At that point it had realised £26,000 (not mentioned in the catalogue). With Christie's able to label it definitively as being by Rubens, the drawing, depicting 'two men being dragged down by demons and being lifted up by three partly robed figures, after Michelangelo', went on to make £1.3 million, the second-highest price ever paid for a Rubens drawing – no doubt questions would have been asked about this colossal difference in much higher places!

⁂

Mechanical Marvel

This year the Sotheby's 'Treasures' sale topped its previous record with a tidy £12 million in just 47 lots. There were some pretty exquisite objects and furniture items featured in the auction, as you might imagine, but one lot that particularly caught my eye was a marvellous mechanical automaton mouse attributed to the Swiss clock maker and mechanician Henri Maillardet (1745–1830). Known as the 'Siberian Mouse', the exterior of this little mechanical marvel comprises a gold body enamelled in faux fur and set with half pearls, bristle whiskers, a gold mesh tail and ruby set eyes. When wound and activated by a little button under the tail, it scuttles around, stops, nibbles and sniffs the air. Given that it was made in 1805, it's a pretty enthralling little object. It sold for £365,000. For a time, Sotheby's had a video of it in action on their website – alas, it has since been taken down. However, fired by the intricate and beautiful history and craftsmanship of this clockwork mouse, I decided to look a little further afield to see just how far the skills of such artisans went. To be honest, over the years, I've been party to the sale of many mechanical singing bird music boxes and automata. The market seems to be strong for high-quality examples and I've seen some good results coming through the salerooms this year. However, the best that are likely to ever come to market must be the two 'Singing Bird Pistols' attributed to the Swiss maker Frères Rochat (the company are still in business making superb automata). Offered by Christie's in 2011, they were catalogued as:

> The only publicly known matching pair of mirror-image gold, enamel, agate, pearl and diamond-set singing bird pistols, made for the Chinese Market, Circa 1820.

To be frank, my descriptive powers can do little to convey the staggering work in these automata. In fact, I'm not going to try. My advice is to head to YouTube, search for 'singing bird pistols' and see for yourself.★ It really is worth it. They sold for a huge $5,866,499 – that's how good they are!

★ Or the link is www.youtube.com/watch?v=KGZRWk51_fU

Another intricate and ingenious automaton sold in 2010 was the 'Ethiopian Caterpillar'. This too was made by Maillardet, again, probably for the Chinese Qianlong court. It's one of seven or eight examples known to exist, with others already in the famous Maurice Sandoz Collection and in the Patek Philippe Museum. In fact, this one too made it into the Sandoz Collection. The mechanics of the caterpillar allow it to propel itself across a surface using a clever concertina motion. Like the pistols and mouse, it is exquisitely fashioned from enamelled gold set with gems. It too can be viewed on YouTube – search for 'automaton silkworm'.★

The caterpillar sold for $415,215 and given the rarity of these incredible 200-year-old 'robots' it seemed unlikely that another would come up for sale. However, in 2013 that's exactly what happened. The example offered in the Sotheby's 'Treasures, Princely Taste' auction realised a little less at $349,392 – yet, that's not the end of it, for this year another one came up for sale in a Sotheby's New York 'Fine Watches' auction, this time in a previously unknown colour variation. It made $262,000 but was evidently in worse condition than the previous examples.

As a footnote to this, Maillardet's skill and fame in creating automata was also enhanced by his promotional use of exhibitions and his inventions were taken as far

---

★ The link is www.youtube.com/watch?v=ZRa3zlrcnKU

afield as America and Russia. One such an exhibition was held at the New Gothic Hall, Haymarket, London, where a masterful creation called 'The Juvenile Artist' or 'Draughtsman-Writer' is known to have been exhibited. It is an immensely complicated and clever automaton of a seated figure that sits at a table, upon which it draws and writes. Built in London in 1800, the figure, now housed in the Franklin Institute in Philadelphia, served as the inspiration for Brian Selznick's book *The Invention of Hugo Cabret*, which in turn was adapted for Martin Scorsese's film *Hugo*.

In fact, the whereabouts of this famous antique android had been lost to history until 1928 when the Philadelphia Institute were given a badly damaged 'machine' which had been in a fire. The donors knew that in times past it had been able to write but it wasn't until after it was restored and demonstrated that it penned the line 'Ecrit par l'Automate de Maillardet'. To be honest I don't think this needs translating. This automaton is a marvel to behold. It draws a number of pictures and writes several poems and if you thought I was saving the best until last then you are absolutely correct. By now, you should already have YouTube open – search 'Maillardet automaton' or 'seven renderings of Maillardet automaton'★ and be prepared to be thoroughly amazed. I was.

★ www.youtube.com/watch?v=Tv5U_fEvrMA

Drawings by the Juvenile Artist.

Spice Trade

The British Museum recently held an exhibition called 'Connecting Continents: Indian Ocean Trade and Exchange'. One of the exhibits was a model boat. Although the date of construction was uncertain (I thought it was 19th century), the Indonesian boat was particularly unusual as its construction was completely derived from cloves. In order for it to be included in the exhibition it had to be cleaned and restored as there were a number of broken and detached elements – mainly figures. Apparently, the conservator said that it still smelt overpoweringly strong. It required 34 hours of painstaking repairs and 'dusting'.

Silver Screen Siren

Marilyn Monroe continues to woo collectors with her iconic, enigmatic, movie-star allure. The bronze marker from her grave was recently offered in an online sale by Julien's Auctions in their Beverly Hills 'Hollywood Legends' sale. The plaque, cast with her name and the dates 1926–1962, was removed from her grave in Westwood Village Memorial Park Cemetery in Los Angeles in the 1970s, due to excessive wear caused by the constant touching of visitors. It was kept in the collection of a former employee of Gasser-Olds, the company who cast the plaque. It sold for

$212,500 on an estimate of $2,000–4,000. I think the professional appraiser (American for valuer) must have been on leave the day that one came in!

Going, Going, Gone

When it comes to big hitting items, Beverly Hills is definitely the undisputed centre of the film memorabilia world. Another screen siren, Vivien Leigh, was represented by the sale of a dress from the highest grossing film ever (once adjusted for inflationary purposes), *Gone With the Wind*. In her acclaimed role as Scarlett O'Hara, she can be seen wearing the dress in four pivotal scenes. Billed by Heritage Auctions as 'one of the most important pieces of memorabilia from the film ever to come up for auction', it realised $137,000. It's a lot of money but somehow it doesn't quite feel like enough … A suit worn by Clark Gable in his role as Rhett Butler made $55,000.

Case Study

Louis Vuitton – it's an iconic brand symbolised by its internationally recognised *LV* monogram. Founded in 1854 by Louis Vuitton, he exploited a gap in the luxury luggage market by producing trunks that stacked. Initially using different designs of canvas to cover the trunks and cases, the famous *LV* and quatrefoil motifs were patented and launched in 1896 and these are the logos that have become synonymous with one of the world's biggest luxury goods brands. I've filmed a few antique pieces over the years on the *Antiques Roadshow* and good trunks are particularly sought by collectors and interior designers. They make excellent coffee tables! To be honest, no foreign holiday would be complete without the usual selection of fake Louis Vuitton bags being proffered by itinerant street salesmen; copying of the brand, as for many other well-known labels, is rife – and of course illegal. However, you're unlikely to ever see a fake cabin trunk! Usually, they hover around the £3,000–5,000 range in the salerooms, depending on the design, and that's exactly what Mander Auctioneers in Sudbury had estimated an example finished in the Damier Ebene pattern (chequered). It was in exceptional condition with an extremely clean and well-fitted interior and as a result realised a commensurate £11,200!

Just the Ticket

It's a niche area of collecting, one that I've written about on other occasions, and it centres around the lovely silver and ivory 'tickets' or tokens that were issued to subscribers of the opera, theatre and races. They were very popular in the 18th and 19th centuries as a form of season ticket and by the nature of the clients that they were issued to, generally belonged to the wealthier side of society. As a result, those that are engraved with the aristocratic names of the rich patrons that purchased them – no doubt for their plush, gilded and velvet-lined opera boxes – can command high prices.

Naturally, I was interested to see that Woolley & Wallis in Salisbury were offering a necklace, the silver gilt chain hung with seven ivory opera tokens, one of which dated from 1831 and was for the Earl of Bristol's box. An interesting reinvention and clever form of upcycling, you might think! Of course, we see all sorts of objects – such as ancient coins – remounted in the same way, but I was also aware that this particular design had a more interesting back story ...

Edith Head, the famous Hollywood costume designer, won eight academy awards over her long and distinguished career. The first, in 1949, was for *The Heiress*, starring Olivia de Havilland; the last was for *The Sting*, in 1973, starring

Paul Newman and Robert Redford. Renowned for her style, Edith had designed and commissioned a gold necklace festooned with thirteen 19th-century ivory tokens, all in circular gold mounts. On her death in 1981, she bequeathed the necklace to her great friend Elizabeth Taylor, and it was subsequently offered by Christie's in 2011 as part of the sale of Taylor's estate. Despite its provenance, the necklace had a derisory estimate of $1,500–2,000. I suspect the gold content alone was worth more than that; the buyers at the sale obviously recognised that it was of far greater worth, given its connections, and it sold for $314,500! Don't for a minute think that this is going to be the marker for the Woolley & Wallis necklace; yet for the £3,000 that their example realised, I felt it was a very affordable nod to two of the great ladies in cinematic history.

Gangster Rap

I've been toying with the purchase of new car for a while. By new, I don't mean brand new, rather 'strange collector's car or eccentric vehicle that I can tinker with'. Unfortunately, some of my more outlandish ideas have been quickly vetoed on the grounds of me being 'too old for that sort of thing' or 'the neighbours will hate you when you start it up'. Possibly, this might have to do with me looking at some rather outrageous hot rods. A big favourite for customising is Ford's Model B, which in 1932 became the first mass-produced car to be fitted with a flathead V8 engine. This 3.6 litre engine produced a fairly measly 65 horsepower, but at the time it was a significant boost and a major milestone in the industry. As it turns out, the Model B – which was itself also commonly known as a V8 (or flathead) – was also Bonnie and Clyde's favourite car.

Bonnie Parker and Clyde Barrow were two of America's most notorious criminals. The couple, along with their gang, wreaked havoc across the central United States during the Great Depression of the early 1930s. During their crime spree they killed at least nine police officers and a number of civilians before they were eventually ambushed and killed in woods near the town of Sailes in Louisiana – in a Ford V8. The glamorisation of their exploits and the legendary status of these carefree killers were very much cemented by the 1967 film *Bonnie & Clyde*, starring Faye Dunaway and Warren Beatty. Yet they were ruthless, no doubt pushed past the point of no return in an all-too-predictable outcome that epitomises the desperate plight of murderous criminals. The actual car can be seen in Whiskey Pete's Casino in Primm, Nevada. It was apparently acquired by the casino for $250,000. Also in the collection is the shirt that Clyde Barrow was wearing when they were ambushed. A hail of 167 bullets hit the car and both Barrow and Parker were killed instantly; he was hit 25 times and she 23. A large quantity of arms was recovered from the car, including a snub-nose .38 calibre revolver, which was found taped to Parker's leg. Barrow's 1911 semi-automatic Colt .45 was similarly found in his waistband and in 2012 the two pistols were sold by RR Auctions in New Hampshire for $260,000 and $240,000 respectively.

Further to this story, there is a letter that was supposedly sent to Henry Ford by Clyde. Its authenticity has often been called into question but it was received at Ford's secretary's office and is stamped for April 1934, the month before they were killed. It reads:

Bonnie and Clyde's bullet-riddled Ford V8.

Tulsa Okla
10th April

Mr. Henry Ford
Detroit Mich

Dear Sir:-

While I still have got breath in my lungs I will tell you
what a dandy car you make. I have drove Fords exclu-
sively when I could get away with one. For sustained
speed and freedom from trouble the Ford has got every
other car skinned and even if my business hasen't [sic]
been strictly legal it don't hurt any thing to tell you
what a fine car you got in the V8 –

Yours truly
Clyde Champion Barrow

Wine Vinegar

Wine has always been an investment commodity. It's traded,
collected, given as a bonus … I'm very partial to a good
glass of wine. I lived in the southwest of France for eight
years, where I developed quite a liking for the sweet varieties of the Jurançon region in the beautiful foothills of the

Pyrenees. My favourites, from the Château de Cabidos and produced by the Nazelle family, are exquisite wines which grace some of the finest lists in the world. I guard a few bottles jealously. In fact, over the years I've stocked a few good vintages in the cellar, although I wince when I think about one bottle that I opened for a special celebration. The wine in question, a 1985 Romanée-Conti, one of the best Burgundies, was corked and tasted like vinegar. Bottles of that vintage generally retail for around £10,000–12,000 in the current market; there have been hefty increases in top-end wine prices, fuelled by Asian buyers. I should have left the cork in it! Bonhams sold a methuselah of the same vintage for £51,770. And just in case you are not sure what a methuselah is, here's a guide to bottle sizes:

Quarter bottle, also known as a piccolo: 187ml (¼ bottle) – 1 glass of wine

Half bottle, demi or split: 375ml (½ bottle) – 2 glasses of wine

Standard: 750ml – the most popular-sized wine bottle offers 4 to 6 glasses of wine

Magnum: 1.5 litres (2 bottles)

Jeroboam or double magnum: 3 litres (4 bottles)

Rehoboam: 4.5 litres (6 bottles)

Bordeaux jeroboam: 5 litres (6⅔ bottles)

Imperial: 6 litres (8 bottles)

Methuselah: 6 litres (8 bottles)★

Salmanazar: 9 litres (12 bottles)

Balthazar: 12 litres (16 bottles)

Nebuchadnezzar: 15 litres (20 bottles)

Melchior: 18 litres (24 bottles)

Solomon: 20 litres (26 bottles)

Sovereign: 25 litres (33⅓ bottles)

Primat or goliath: 27 litres (36 bottles)

Melchizedek: 30 litres (40 bottles)

These following bottle sizes are some of the more obscure variations:

Cylinder: 100ml – 'test tube' bottles used for single servings of Sauternes; this size is also used for some bottles of Essencia from the Tokaji region in Hungary.

Chopine: 250ml (⅓ bottle) – 1¼ glasses, used more often in France.

★ The Imperial and Methuselah have the same capacity but the former is used for Bordeaux, the latter for Champagne.

Clavelin half: 310ml – used for *vin jaune*, the yellow wine of the Jura region of France.

Tenth: 378ml

Jennie: 500ml (⅔ bottle) – this is an uncommon wine bottle size and is mostly used for sweet dessert-style wines from Tokaji, Sauternes and its surrounding regions, or Jerez (sherry).

Clavelin full: 620ml – rarely seen, this wine bottle size is used for *vin jaune*, the yellow wine of the Jura region of France.

Litre: 1,000ml – this wine bottle falls in between a full bottle and a magnum and has been popularised in California by Grace Family Vineyards.

Marie Jeanne: 2.25 litres (3 bottles) – Port producers often refer to this bottle as a Tregnum or Tappit Hen bottle.

Please note that some of these bottles are used very specifically for different wines and champagnes, with some wine producers never exceeding 18-litre bottles.

A Wee Dram

Still on the subject of alcohol (please remember to drink responsibly), I'm also partial to a dram of whisky; I suspect it might have something to do with my Scottish ancestry. I usually keep a selection of about fifteen assorted bottles, all Scottish of course. However, a recent auction purchase added to that selection with the addition of some 500 whisky miniatures which had come from a deceased estate. (I use the spelling 'whisky' because they are all Scottish. 'Whiskey' with an 'e' tends to be reserved for the Irish and American varieties.) I'm not sure what I'm going to do with them as I regard a tipple as a bit of a treat rather than a habit – perhaps a tasting evening might be appropriate. I also recently bought an English whisky (yes, the makers have opted for the Scottish spelling).

The Japanese have always had a passion for whisky and I remember a particularly good Japanese restaurant that I used to frequent in London, where regular businessmen from Japan kept their own labelled bottles in a large cabinet. Given the global rise in interest surrounding fine wines and spirits, I was also interested to see that for the first time a tipple from Japan has been named the best whisky in Jim Murray's *Whisky Bible* – Suntory's Yamazaki Sherry Cask Single Malt, 2013, in the 2015 edition of the book. The malt, limited to 16,500 bottles, will no doubt continue to rocket in price and is already almost impossible to find. In fact, as I'm writing this, one is just finishing on eBay at over €2,000. I've found another retailing for over £2,500.

Whisky has many advantages for both investors and collectors. Once it's out of the cask and bottled, it rarely changes significantly, meaning that your bottle will always be drinkable – unlike the gambling that can occur with wine. Appreciation in value has been consistent and the market has demanded more frequent sales, with salerooms like Bonhams leading the way with four auctions a year in Edinburgh and sales in Hong Kong. They have consistently raised the bar and rare malts have been making more and more over the years. Highlights include the world-record price set in 2011 for a 55-year-old Glenfiddich, which was made to commemorate the 110th birthday of Janet Sheed Roberts, whose grandfather William Grant founded the Glenfiddich Distillery. With only eleven bottles having been released (four more were retained by the family), it made £46,850! That's a pretty expensive tipple!

Holy Hoaxes

I love a relic and I've travelled much of Europe in search of some of the best. However, it's not always necessary to go that far afield when you're after an interesting story and this is one Indiana Jones-type tale that recently caused a bit of a stir in the national press.

The Nanteos Cup is a late medieval mazer bowl that, as legend has it, was fashioned from a piece of the True Cross. The cup, which is badly damaged and of which only around 45 per cent survives, is thought to be fashioned from Wych elm and is fairly typical of medieval mazers or drinking bowls. However, the legend surrounding this bowl has traditionally imbued it with healing powers. The receptacle was kept for many years at Nanteos Mansion, Rhydyfelin, near Aberystwyth in Mid Wales, and appears to have first come into the folkloric tradition of holy relics in 1878 when George Ernest Powell, who inherited the Nanteos estate, exhibited it to the Cambrian Archaeological Society. He was a budding romantic poet and it has been suggested that his propensity for collecting the unusual and the freedom of expression that his inheritance gave him were probably instrumental in his creative assertions about the history of the cup. It seems that the Society's meeting minutes record it as having been 'preserved for many years past at Nanteos' and before that it was understood to have been at the abbey of Strata Florida, a Cistercian establishment founded in 1164 near Tregaron; the abbey was pulled down by Henry VIII in the dissolution of the monasteries (the ruins are still standing). It's quite likely that the cup was excavated at Strata Florida and that it appeared at a time equating with work and excavations taking place at the abbey. Prior to this, as some antiquarians have noted, it seems to have no previous provenance.

Its candidature as the Holy Grail evolved around certain myths that were probably created by Powell. Yet the story surrounding the bowl has, as with many folkloric objects, captured people's imagination, and it recently caused quite a stir when it was stolen from a private residence

North door of Strata Florida Abby.

An 18th-century engraving of the ruins of Strata Florida Abbey.

in June 2014. Apparently, it had been lent for its curative powers to a lady that had gone into hospital; her home was burgled while she was away, leading to a hunt by Mercia Police as part of Operation Icarus, which centres upon the theft and sale of religious artefacts. The story featured on BBC's *Crimewatch*, and at one point a local public house was raided on a warrant with intelligence that the bowl had been sighted there. However, the landlady said that the only object that resembled it in the pub was a salad bowl! The 'Holy Grail' was eventually recovered and handed over in a pre-arranged meeting. A man was arrested but no charges have been pressed.

Muzzle Loader

I own several musket balls, some found with my metal detector and obviously dating from the English Civil War period, others purchased in moments of weakness while trawling eBay. Such examples include a boxed duo from HMS *Invincible*, a captured French 74-gun ship that was lost after hitting a sandbank off the Isle of Wight in 1758. None are valuable or particularly rare but there's something that I can't quite pin down about musket balls – they have a sort of fatal attraction. Two examples that I really would have liked turned up in Lyon & Turnbull's 'Jacobite, Stuart and Scottish Applied Arts' sale. The pair are identically gold-mounted and had reputedly been found on Culloden Moor – who knows, they may even have whizzed past Bonnie Prince Charlie's ears during the battle. I had them pegged as a potentially great pair of 'talking point' cufflinks but they were fired off quickly at a very robust £3,875, including premium.

⁂

Narcotics Bust

Good ethnographic items continue to increase in value and it's interesting to note, particularly from my experience on the *Antiques Roadshow*, that it's not unusual to see a good indigenous native club or artefact snaking along the queue towards my miscellaneous table. The reason for this is our nation's colonial history. With such a long and often nefarious record of imperialist domination and religious suppression, our ancestors acquired many souvenirs of their conquests and occupations. For this reason, good items seem to continue to turn up at auction. It's also an area that requires some very specific knowledge, and it's unusual for auction houses without a specialist department to be able to identify such a varied cross-section of material.

In essence, this is why many people go to salerooms, to pick up on some of these deficiencies, yet in reality, errors in knowledge and cataloguing don't always lead to a bargain. One such example was the kava bowl offered by High Road Auctions in Chiswick. Not to be confused with cava, that well-known Spanish sparkling wine, kava is a plant grown in the western Pacific, the roots of which are used to produce a narcotic drink that has relaxant and sedative properties. Known as yaqona in Fiji, it is a muddy-looking liquid and 19th-century accounts liken its effect to a strong muscle relaxant that causes a mild paralysis without affecting the brain. Its use as a ceremonial preparation probably dates over a couple of millennia. Even the Queen has sampled it on visits to the western Pacific. It is traditionally served in a large wooden dish with integrally carved legs, which looks like a low table. These are still made and touristy examples can be purchased as decorative objects for relatively small amounts of money.

However, at their best, the rarest examples of these bowls take the form of turtles and in 2011 Sotheby's in New York offered a particularly fine example with a good provenance. Thought to have been carved from the wood of the sacred vesi tree, the colour and patination suggested that it had seen extensive ritual use which largely predated its early 20th-century museum connections. Although estimated at \$100,000–150,000 it topped this easily at \$326,500, including the premium. The Chiswick example was not quite in the same league and was meagrely esti-mated at £40–60. No doubt bidders were keeping things close to their chests prior to the sale and there was no doubt that it was a 19th-century example. In the end, it made a quite notable £4,800.

Record Record

I've got some great psychedelic records in my vinyl col-lection. To be honest, some of them I bought just for the mind-bending covers, although some I would lay claim to having purchased for their experimental use of early electronic instruments such as the Mellotron, an electro-mechanical tape-keyboard instrument, or the Theremin, a strange instrument developed in the late 1920s by Russian Léon Theremin, that controls the pitch of two high-powered oscillators by the movement of the performer's hands – in mid-air! Of course, the whole nature of psyche-delia was a spin-off of the drugs culture of the 1960s and the use of LSD as advocated by the famous alternative

American psychologist Timothy Leary. Most major bands of the period dabbled – if not fully embraced – psyche-delic culture, including The Beatles, yet the culture also influenced just about every genre of music and art in that period, a history far too diverse and complicated to cover in depth here.

Among the more obscure records in my collection is one by The Troll, a Chicago-based four-piece band that had two drummers. Their one and only album, *Animated Music*, has some great trippy rock/vaudeville crossovers – perhaps not everybody's cup of tea! Of course, values vary enormously but what is the most valuable psyche-delic LP? Well, one of the rarest is *Tinkerbell's Fairydust* by Tinkerbell's Fairydust, a short-lived British band that released three singles prior to the release of the album in 1969 – the LP was withdrawn at the last moment and, apart from a few test pressings, only a few finished cop-ies survived the withdrawal. It's now regarded as one of the most valuable 'pop/psych' albums ever made. Special Auction Services in Berkshire recently offered one and it sold for a mind-altering £2,300.

Blackboard Scribble

It's been another blockbuster year of show-stopping prices for modern art. Christie's notched up their highest grossing auction ever at their Contemporary Art sale in New York with a massive $852.9 million. This was in contrast to a still good, but slightly disappointing sale held by Sotheby's the night before, which came in a little under its projected estimate with $343.7 million. Both sales set some impressive records for contemporary artists and although some works were relatively fresh to the market, others saw massive gains within just a few years of last appearing.

Sotheby's offerings were led by a Mark Rothko dating from 1951, which topped the proceedings at $44.97 million. Readers of *Allum's Antiques Almanac 2015* may remember that I painted a 'Rothko' of my own – now hanging in my garden shed and currently valued at around £20. Christie's previous record saleroom total had stood at $745 million, achieved only seven months earlier; this latest record-breaker raised the bar even further, and included two Warhols: *Triple Elvis* (1963) and *Four Marlons*, which sold for $81.9 million and $69.6 million respectively. Apparently, the mood was such in the saleroom that people were either struck dumb or unimpressed with the second figure and forgot to clap! (Frankly, that's more of an American thing anyway.) Interestingly, these two lots had both been guaranteed by Christie's, so there was relatively little worry about them selling.

The third-highest achiever was one of Cy Twombly's 'blackboard' paintings, a large example of this series executed between 1966 and 1971. Although late on in the period, *Untitled* was signed and dated 1970 verso and was heavily backed-up in the 'Post-Lot Text' with a 2,300-word critique and explanation. It makes for interesting reading and is well worth a look, for it is everything you might want to hate about the modern art world and at the same time everything that makes it so enthralling and enigmatic! Anyway, the lot easily surpassed its estimate (again guaranteed by Christie's) to make a record-breaking $69,605 million!

On this occasion, I'll refrain from trying to knock one up in the garden shed.

Flayed Alive!

In 1543 one of the most groundbreaking books in human anatomy was published: *De humani corporis fabrica*. The writer, Andreas Vesalius (1514–1564), professor of the school of medicine at Padua, gained fame and fortune in

Europe as a result. At the age of 28, this was a monumental achievement in both the understanding of the human body and the magnificent and accurate portrayal of human anatomy in over 250 superb woodblock engravings. Vesalius' approach to anatomy and dissection meant that his hands-on anatomical lectures involved him directly in the dissection of bodies, a practice which apparently was normally undertaken with the direction of the doctor and a barber-surgeon. This personal involvement enabled Vesalius to have a much greater understanding of the body and across the seven volumes of the work he split it into the following sections:

1. The Bones and Cartilages
2. The Ligaments and Muscles
3. The Veins and Arteries
4. The Nerves
5. The Organs of Nutrition and Generation
6. The Heart and Associated Organs
7. The Brain

The woodblock illustrations, regarded as some of the finest ever produced and attributed to the 'The Studio of Titian', were immensely expensive. Vesalius dedicated the work to Charles V, the Holy Roman Emperor. In fact, Vesalius presented the first copy to Charles V, the

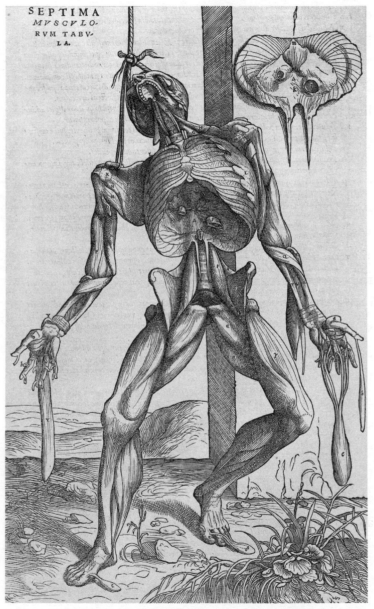

A plate from Book II: The Ligaments and Muscles.

only hand-coloured edition to be made – bound in purple silk velvet! This actual copy was sold by Christie's in 1998 as part of the Haskell F. Norman library. It sold for $1.5 million. Vesalius was subsequently appointed as the Emperor's personal physician.

There are relatively few complete surviving copies, although one such work in Brown University, Rhode Island, is bound in human skin, a not altogether uncommon practice for the period. The 'art' of binding books with human skin is known as anthropodermic bibliopegy and this macabre procedure was often implemented using the skin of felons and murderers. The Bristol Records Office also owns such an example, a volume bound in the skin of one John Horwood, an eighteen-year-old who was hanged for the murder of a woman called Eliza Balsam in 1821. The tome contains notes on the case and states that after Horwood's body was publicly dissected by the surgeon Richard Smith at Bristol Royal Infirmary, the doctor directed that his skin be tanned for this very purpose. Gruesome!

The latest copy of Vesalius' masterpiece to surface – again offered by Christie's – was sold for $300,000.

Newsflash

*Napoleon complex is a pejorative term describing
a disproven psychological condition which is said
to exist in people, both men and women, of short
stature. It is also known as 'Napoleonic complex'.*
—Wikipedia

I know – you think I've got a Napoleon fixation; but quite apart from my love of the history surrounding the man, it's interesting to see how the vagaries of the market can dictate hugely different sums of money for objects that look or seem to be intrinsically similar. I've written elsewhere about the example of Napoleon's hat selling for £1.5 million (*see* 'Bicorn or Tricorn', *page 126*); after that I was keen to see what the next one to reach the market was going to sell for – and several months later I found out.

Christie's, like most major auction houses, have certainly upped their game over the years. Clever branding and marketing of sales has turned out to be a feature of the auction circuit and Christie's annual 'Extraordinary' sale has attracted massive attention in the media for its eclectic selection of unusual and iconic historic lots. This year was no different and, keen to cash in on the Waterloo bicentenary, their offerings included several pieces directly from the collection of Sir Michael Shaw Stewart, a Scottish baronet who at the age of 27 went on the obligatory Grand Tour of Europe in 1814. As a consequence, he developed a bit of an interest in Napoleon and acquired several artefacts on his travels, including a hat, complete with musket ball hole, worn by Napoleon at the battle of Friedland in 1807. At the time it cost ten Thalers, which is apparently around £2 in the money of the day. Stewart also tried to meet Napoleon but was unlucky, although he was fortunate enough to meet his mother, Letizia Bonaparte, who gave him a portrait of the Emperor by the famous historical painter Robert Lefèvre. (Deprived of his patronage after the 1830 revolution, Lefèvre committed suicide by cutting his own throat at the age of 55.)

The hat, much vaunted by the press to make at least £500,000, was probably overcooked following the success of the previous year's sale to Korean chicken magnate Kim Hong-Kuk, and the Christie's estimate of £300,000–500,000 was more sensible. As it transpired it realised £386,500, including commission. The portrait did somewhat better, surpassing its £600,000 bottom estimate to make £842,500 all in.

Just to emphasise the diversity of the extraordinary lots in this auction, in the same sale a Supermarine Spitfire P9347, one of only two MK1 Spitfires restored to flying condition, was sold by the art collector and philanthropist Thomas Kaplan for a world-record £3,106,500, the proceeds going to the RAF Benevolent Fund and several wildlife charities. Another show-stopping piece was a Luba figure from the Democratic Republic of Congo. Dating from around 1880, the female figure, carved for a bow stand, carried a very good provenance and exhibition record, and set the second-highest price ever for an African work of art at auction; at £6,130,500 it will take some beating!

Burnt Offering

One of my favourite publications is *Current Archaeology*. Every month I look forward to the latest edition dropping through the letterbox. There are those who criticise (having obviously not read the magazine), saying that British archaeology is boring to read about because there's never anything interesting dug up, just potsherds and waterlogged wood – which couldn't be further from the truth. Just look at the Staffordshire Hoard! I, along with many others, regard *CA* as essential bedtime reading.

Forgive me if I've said this before but my interest does stem from being a frustrated would-be archaeologist. Frankly, my knees are probably not up to it any more but it was with great enthusiasm that I was recently able, with the help of local archaeologist and historian Mike Stone, to conduct a dig in the front garden of my own house.

Basically, I live on a very historic site in the town of Chippenham. There have been settlers here since at least Roman times; we know this because Roman remains have been found in several places around the town (indeed, we found Roman pottery in my front garden!). However, Chippenham's main claim to fame comes in the form of its Saxon history. My house is the old rectory. Prior to that it was a medieval wool merchant's and burgess's house. I have the title of Freeman of Chippenham, as my house still carries the association. It's built in a strategic place on a raised area within a large bow of the River Avon – it's a good defensive position. My home is located next to St Andrew's Church, and it was here, on this site, that King Alfred's sister Ethelswitha was married to the King of Mercia in 853. Alfred was only four years old at the time. The site was known as a royal parish or 'vill', and subsequently Alfred's palace (or stronghold) was situated here also. However, these were turbulent times and in 878 the Viking king Guthrum besieged Alfred at Chippenham, taking advantage of the Christmas festivities, and Alfred was forced to flee, narrowly escaping down to the Somerset Levels. Later that same year, Alfred returned, besieged and defeated Guthrum at the battle of Edington and as a result of that defeat Guthrum accepted Alfred's terms to be baptised and become Christian. This agreement was known as the 'Treaty of Wedmore' or the 'Treaty of Chippenham'. Although historical references to this treaty are scant, Guthrum obviously made an agreement with Alfred that led to peace and his own return to East Anglia, to an area which became known as the Danelaw, which in real terms gave Guthrum sway over the east and north of England. Although the term was not really a geographical one – it simply meant an area over which the law of the Danes was enforced – it equated to about a third of the English kingdoms, which in turn were later conquered by the English kings. So, given this incredible history, it's quite amazing to think that I live on a site where some of this took place. Digging it up was a no-brainer.

The first dig took place in my front garden and the supposition was that we might find traces of the Saxon defensive ditch that bordered Alfred's enclosure. Sadly we didn't. We did, however, find hundreds of objects dating from the 19th century right through to the Roman period. I gave everything to our wonderful local museum in Chippenham, which was probably a bit of a headache for them but a good display was arranged for a few months. Now, as I write, we are gearing up to dig up an area of the back garden in the hope that we might find some really definitive evidence of Alfred's occupation.

I feel that it's time for Alfred's presence in the town to

be recognised and I'm very keen to start a fund to have a statue or monument erected. I think I'll have to start a committee ... In the meantime, just in case you were wondering about the famous 'burnt cakes' legend when Alfred, having been given shelter by a peasant woman, took his eye off the baking and burnt the cakes – it's most likely a 19th-century invention! Funnily enough, there's an edible type of fungus known as King Alfred's Cakes – *Daldinia concentrica* mainly grows on ash and beech, and has a black, burnt appearance.

Meiji Marvel

As a collector, I seem to steer more towards Japanese works of art than Chinese. I think the main reason for this personal preference is the exquisite intricacy that characterises many Japanese items; the craftsmanship of some disciplines is so intensely complex, convoluted and time-consuming that it's sometimes hard to imagine how such skills and technology existed so many centuries ago. Strangely, despite these qualities, many Japanese works of art remain relatively affordable (in relation to Chinese items), largely due to the fact that the Japanese market still remains depressed.

One area of intricacy that always fascinates me is the

decoration on Satsuma pottery. The earliest Satsuma wares date from the late 17th century but they were not elaborately decorated in the way that most people understand Satsuma; rather they were quite plain dark pottery wares that were used domestically. Richly decorated Satsuma on a buff-ivory coloured ground is actually a 19th-century invention, mostly from the Meiji period of 1868–1912. At its best, Satsuma ware is exquisite but, as with many genres, the style and quality was ultimately corrupted by demand from the West and the production of crude designs which appealed to the mass market but not to the connoisseur. In reality, Satsuma was never made for home consumption and was apparently seen by many as a 'betrayal of Japanese tradition'. What is certain is that as a product, it was designed to appeal to Western consumers. Its adaptation to those consumers' styles too, rather than retaining a purely Japanese aesthetic, resulted in some interesting – if not 'pure' – Art Deco Satsuma pieces that blend the geometric designs of the 1920s and 30s with this distinctive Japanese form of pottery and decoration.

As the production of Satsuma expanded in the 19th century, its manufacture was no longer confined to the region after which it is named. Various workshops and studios sprang up across Japan, the most famous and prolific being that of Kinkōzan – the brand that I see the most of when I am out and about valuing. There were many others too but I was fascinated to see that a rather lovely example had appeared at Gorringes Auctioneers bearing the mark of Taizan. This pottery was formed in 1673 and is highly renowned for its quality products. This twelve-inch dish was fabulously decorated with a highly intricate scene of a ship surrounded by silk traders tossing skeins of silk from the decks. Although estimated at a rather shy £600–800, probably due to the market conditions, it made a much healthier £10,500! Interestingly, it was sold to an American buyer, echoing the route of earlier Taizan pieces, which were mainly exported to the USA after about 1873. The company went out of business in 1922.

Here Pussy Pussy

The opening titles on the *Antiques Roadshow* last approximately 35 seconds. Within that very short space of time a fictional story is played out about the incredible lengths people might be prepared to go to in order to get their items to a show. Over the years there has been a Citroën 2CV with a longcase clock sticking out of the roof and a more apt British Morris Minor with a suit of armour similarly positioned. However, the most recent set of titles were destined to break the mould a little when I was asked to help with the production of a new sequence.

Given that I live in an interesting house in a picturesque street it seemed like a good idea to utilise various aspects of the locality to set the scene for some new titles. A motorcycle had already been decided as the main mode of transport. In previous sequences buses, boats and bicycles had all been used. We thought a boat might be interesting so we called upon a neighbour to motor up and down the river just over the road from my house, with one of my Georgian portraits and my dog on board. We also included my cat, Minou, a lovely moggy I rescued out in France; at one point he negotiates a tabletop full of objects, causing a vase to wobble. That shot required a few takes, aided by a bag of tasty treats!

Using the wonders of modern technology, a beautiful Queen Anne house over the road from my home was opened up like a dolls house and filled with the contents of a real Victorian one. The suit of Japanese samurai armour revealed in the modern garage is the one that resides in my library, and the little boy who stares in wonder at the row of medals was filmed in the loft of my barn – we dressed it with a few fake cobwebs and props! There are various other elements from my collection also included in the sequence and it was great fun to do. The wonderful wrought-iron gates through which the motorcycle passes are at Tredegar House in Newport, a National Trust property where we filmed two wonderful shows and the Art Deco plaster mannequin's head in the motorcycle sidecar lives in my bathroom. So, next time you watch the show take a concentrated look – it's amazing how much you can pack into 35 seconds!

❦

Feathers or Kapok?

Cushions are an everyday decorative feature of our lives; in fact they come in such an incredible variety of shapes, sizes and designs that there's a cushion to suit every epoch and style that you can possibly imagine. Given that they vary in size too, larger formats in particular can be used in their own right as furniture – the bean bag, for example. Historically, they are probably one of the oldest forms of portable furniture. They are mentioned throughout history in both religious and secular situations and have also been important symbolically for royalty too. Cushions for specific uses, such as 'bible cushions' or the distinctive red or crimson, gold-tasselled cushions known as 'royal pillows', would commonly be used for presentation, prayer or for carrying ceremonial objects.

However, the cushion as art might seem like a step too far. I'm not referring to the thousands of cushions that are available printed with art images (a quick look on the internet will illustrate just how many works of art are featured on cushions these days). I am referring to the idea that the cushion itself can be purposely made as a work of art.

Grayson Perry is perhaps one of the most controversial and arguably one of the most interesting British modern artists currently working. My favourite Perry works are his pottery – I love his gritty take on contemporary life and issues, his shameless comments on all aspects of society and the way he mixes up everything from medievalism to modernity both in his technique and content. His tapestries are another such vehicle that forces the observer to decipher complex artistic anagrams, yet, when they are revealed they seem so obvious that Perry's sense of humour is quite shamelessly playing with the bystander – I love them! One such work, *The Walthamstow Tapestry*, is a clever comment on man's dependence, from birth to death, on the power of consumerism and branding. At fifteen metres by three metres, it's an imposing work and quite obviously a valuable piece of art too … so how much would a cushion-sized fragment be worth?

The answer to that question was resolved at Roseberys Auctioneers in London when a cushion measuring 43cm square, made from a fragment of *The Walthamstow Tapestry*, came up for auction. Apparently it was created as a test piece for the main work and given to the vendor by Perry. The LEGO brand name featured prominently within the design. It sold for £4,200, so, if I quickly work out that the main tapestry has a surface area roughly equivalent to 94 (double-sided) cushions, that would mean a total value of £394,800. Crude perhaps, but interesting nonetheless; in reality, only small works by Perry seem to come up for sale, so there is not really any precedent for such large tapestries ... who knows what they are actually worth? At any rate, it's a large price for a cushion and probably not one you'd want to lounge on.

Lunar Love

I own the odd meteorite and I recently had fun filming some NASA space-flown circuitry on the *Antiques Roadshow*. It's an area that fascinates me, no doubt fostered by memories of my father making sure I was up in time to watch the first moon landing – I was just five years old. Space-related items have continued to attract strong but selective interest in the collecting world, although it's not just 20th-century material from those space-race years of my youth that attract attention.

The earliest representations of our celestial knowledge are eagerly sought by both collectors and museums and one such masterpiece to recently come up for sale at Sotheby's in Paris was Jean-Dominique Cassini's *Carte de la Lune* of 1679. Born in Italy in 1625, Cassini changed his name from Giovanni Domenico Cassini in 1673. His French-friendly name came about as a consequence of being invited to Paris by Louis XIV in 1669. Cassini's reputation had preceded him and his groundbreaking work in astronomy had resulted in various breakthroughs such as calculating the positions of Jupiter's moons and computing the rotation of Mars to within two-and-a-half minutes of our modern equivalent. He became a member of the Académie Royale des Sciences and was the director of the Observatoire de Paris.

His *Carte de la Lune* is one of his most incredible feats. After eight years of study through a telescope, and with the assistance of Sébastien Leclerc and Jean Partigny on the preparatory drawings, he was able to complete a map of the moon that was unrivalled in its accuracy for the next 200 years. Engravings of the *Carte de la Lune* are incredibly rare, with only half a dozen known to exist. The Observatoire de Paris still has 57 of the original drawings, as well as a copy of the map. The recent Sotheby's example sold for £67,455.

Cassini's *Carte de la Lune* – can you spot Geneviève?

As an interesting footnote, in 1673 Cassini married a lady called Geneviève de Laistre. He clearly loved her, for within the engraving he included the image of a woman on the Promontory of Héraclides and a heart in the Sea of Serenity. The woman is said to be Geneviève.

Freeze Dried

The Bonhams 'Space History' sale that took place in New York this year emphasised the selective nature of the space market. On the surface of it the auction promised much, with some more than interesting items ranging from photographs and rare space-flown artefacts to meteorites, space suits, prototype models, training equipment and the personal effects of astronauts.

Several lots were included belonging to Alan LaVern Bean, who flew his first mission on Apollo 12 in 1969 and was the fourth person to walk on the moon; one comprising several pouches of space-flown food and two spoons mounted in a slightly cheesy gilt frame was estimated at $50,000–80,000. There was also a 'life support strap' catalogued as being 'Soiled With Lunar Dust' at £60,000–90,000. Along with other lots, these estimates seemed punchy, even for such historically associated items and the room decided similarly – the unsold rate for the sale was high, with lots being selectively cherry-picked. One such 'cherry' was Bean's 18-carat gold Omega Speedmaster Chronograph. Space-flown watches are incredibly desirable and very valuable. This example had not been out of our atmosphere but had been presented to Bean as one of a series of 30 that were given to President Nixon, his Vice-President Agnew, and the Apollo astronauts. It was engraved verso:

—Astronaut Alan Bean—
to mark man's conquest of space
with time, through time, on time.
Skylab Mission II [III]
Apollo 12.

The watch sold for $50,000, the highest selling lot in the sale.

⁂

American Realist

John Singleton Copley (1738–1815) is regarded as one of America's most important early colonial painters. Born to Anglo-Irish parents, possibly in Boston, Massachusetts, as well as working in America he spent some 40 years in Britain and Europe. He is renowned for his realist portraits and the accurate and attentive portrayal of his subjects, with interesting objects in the compositions. His fame in English circles was cemented by his admittance to the Society of Artists of Great Britain after the exhibition of his painting *Boy with a Squirrel*, a charming work that depicts his half-brother Henry Pelham playing with a pet squirrel. He painted many prominent personalities and aristocrats of the day and was also renowned for his historical depictions. Quite understandably, his work is very sought after in the States, although his back catalogue, which amounts to perhaps some 350 works, is mainly held by institutions and museums, including the Smithsonian.

Although several works have come to auction over the last decade or so, the most significant was a portrait of Mrs Theodore Atkinson Junior (1765), acquired by the Crystal Bridges Museum of American Art in Arkansas, a project financed by the Wal-Mart billionairess Alice Walton. It made just shy of £2 million. Perhaps one of his most famous or revered works is a self-portrait in the Smithsonian. It has a freedom of expression and vibrancy so suggestively and loosely brushed that it is almost unparalleled in the period (my opinion!). So, it was with international interest that two pencil and charcoal drawings that were thought to be self-portraits by Copley were offered by Cheffins Auctioneers. They were reputedly from an Irish country house, always a good draw, and were executed on paper. They realised £6,000, which seems very reasonable value to me. Assuming that they are fully provenanced and confirmed as works by Copley, I would imagine that they will make a much-coveted addition to any collection.

An Enigma

Alan Turing OBE, FRS (1912–1954) was a brilliant pioneering scientist, mathematician and leading protagonist in the field of theoretical computer science and artificial intelligence. His work during the Second World War was highly significant in both the part it played in shortening the war and the advancement of computer technology. Turing was at Bletchley Park where he worked for the Government Code and Cypher School. His job was basically to break codes, an important part of the British intelligence drive to defeat the Nazis. A Polish invention designed to crack the German Enigma machine codes had been created by Marian Rejewski around 1938. The device, called the 'bomba kryptologiczna' – or, translated from the Polish, 'cryptologic bomb' – was an electromechanical machine that could do the work of 100 human codebreakers. It was a startlingly clever invention, which Turing and his team built upon to make the British version, a machine which when used in quantity (200 were in use by the end of the war) made a massive difference to the Allies' capabilities in cracking what the Germans thought were safely transmitted codes. Turing's theorems were vital in the design of the machine, which undoubtedly saved many lives in helping to bring the war to an earlier close. His life and involvement are portrayed in the

2014 film *The Imitation Game*, in which his part is played by Benedict Cumberbatch.

Sadly, Turing's life and achievements were later blighted by society's intolerant attitude towards homosexuality. He became embroiled in a relationship with a man that ended badly and he was prosecuted for gross indecency under the laws of the time. He was given a choice: imprisonment or a course of hormonal treatment. He accepted the latter, which effectively neutered him; a cruel and dreadful sentence. His conviction precluded him from doing other vital security work, as his clearances were removed. He was also unable to enter the USA, although he kept his academic job. In essence, what the paranoia and bigotry of the time did was to largely rob us of one of the greatest minds of the 20th century. He was found dead in his home in 1954. Although the autopsy gave a verdict of suicide by cyanide poisoning, there are many who think that his death was an accidental poisoning caused by chemicals that he was experimenting with.

However, Turing is now recognised for the man that he was: a great logician, mathematician, philosopher and scientist. In 2009, following a national campaign, the prime minister, Gordon Brown, made a public apology for the way that the British Government had treated him. The Queen posthumously pardoned him in 2013. Since his death, and particularly as a result of events surrounding the centenary of his birth in 2013, Turing is now remembered with the respect that he so rightly deserves. He is now commemorated through many awards and tributes. As a result of his important place in history, objects associated with him are also highly sought after.

This year, his notebook dating from 1942, penned during his work at Bletchley Park and entrusted to fellow mathematician Robin Gandy, sold for $1 million at Bonhams in New York. Recently, a letter sent by Turing to the eight-year-old daughter of his analyst, explaining how to crack the game of solitaire, sent just a year before he died, sold for £40,000 at Bonhams London. Value of the artefacts aside, our acknowledgement does not come down to the monetary value of the objects that he left behind. Turing's legacy is priceless.

❧❦❧

Einstein A-go-go

In my book *The Collector's Cabinet*, I discuss the whereabouts of Albert Einstein's brain – an 'artefact' that will never come up for sale. However, items associated with the great scientist occasionally do arrive at auction and there have been a few interesting results lately. Early or personally signed photographs of Einstein are rare. In 1992, an image taken in 1924 with an inscription related to the ideal of a Jewish homeland sold for a whopping $60,000. Hopes were consequently high for another photograph recently offered, taken in 1921 on Einstein's first trip to the United States. His visit was primarily to raise money for the new Hebrew University of Jerusalem which had been founded some three years earlier. Inscribed in German on the border, the words make reference to a 'splendid campaigner for our university' but it's not known to whom he gave the photograph. It was sold by Christie's in New York for a very respectable $30,000.

Another interesting memento was offered by RR Auctions in the form of a Red Star Line postcard from the liner *Belgenland*, on which he took his only visit to Palestine in 1923. As well as an inscription, Einstein has drawn two caricatures on the front of the card, one of himself and another of his friend Hanna Ruppin. The card realised $45,000.

The most expensive lot, however, was an eight-page draft of a scientific paper related to UFT (unified field theory – don't ask me to explain it!). Written around 1930, it sold for $150,000.

Mythical Beasts

The other day, as you do, I was thumbing through one of a number of amazing 16th-century tomes that had been saved from a skip. I know what you are thinking – the old skip story again. These were delivered to me in two shopping bags in order that I might give my humble opinion as to their potential value. By all accounts they had belonged to a distant relative who had left Germany before the outbreak of the Second World War. Having passed away, his possessions were being sorted out and on clearing the house these books had been saved from being consigned to the skip, because they looked interesting. Apparently, there were others that met that fate – which doesn't bear thinking about.

Anyway, my favourite of the bunch was a leather-bound monster by one Adamus Lonicerus (1528–1586), a German botanist and physician, and known as a *Kräuterbuch* – in English it would be known as a 'herbal'. Published in four editions between 1557 and 1577, this one being a 1577 edition, it's quite difficult to describe on paper how it feels when turning the pages of such a book. At over 400 years old, it bears the notes and scribblings of previous owners and its pages are profusely illustrated – many hand-coloured (probably later). It encompasses all sorts of areas of life and mortality. For me, the wonder in reading such a book is very much about the associations of alchemy, early scientific discovery, mythology and the chasm between what was understood in the 16th century (or not) and the way it is so innocently recorded. There are pages of designs for stills and instructions for the distilling of herbs and potions, a hugely comprehensive field guide to herbs and plants, and a marvellous illustrated catalogue of the 'living terrestrial creatures', naturally commencing with a wonderful woodblock of Adam and Eve. Among the many stylised representations of exotic animals including tigers, lions, camels and monkeys are the more mundane creatures: a delightfully spiteful-looking rat and, on the mythological front (to us, that is), the magical and rarely seen unicorn and griffin.

But best of all are the amazing sections on *Steins Bezoar* or Bezoar stones, the 'magical' 'stones' found in the

The elusive unicorn.

gastrointestinal tracts of many creatures around the world and thought to be the antidote to all poisons. Certainly in this period they were highly prized and the section relating to them is illustrated by a woodblock of stags, one being bitten on the nose by a serpent – no doubt a reference to poison.

Even more enthralling is the section on mummies, or more specifically 'mumia', a substance used in mummification, much valued for its medicinal properties. Usually bitumen- or asphalt-based, this substance was used by the Egyptians and as such, ancient mummies were highly prized, and were ground up to make medicinal preparations. The demand was so great in the medieval period that recently deceased corpses were often embalmed in order that there would be mumia of sorts to harvest at a later

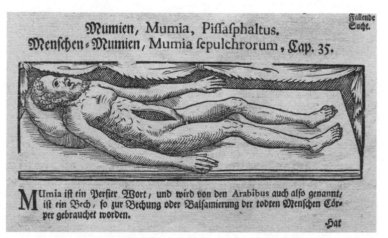

How to mummify a corpse, 16th-century style.

date – this was known as *mumia falsa*, an inferior preparation to the ancient variety.

In case you haven't guessed, the word 'mummy' has its origins in the term 'mumia'.

This, among the several other tomes I have been pondering, is probably worth around £2,000–3,000. It's a gem.

Ivory Queen

The vagaries of auction are sometimes hard to explain – there are so many variables. Results are often unpredictable and items that remain unsold on one occasion can supersede their original expectations when re-offered. Being a bit of an internet sleuth, I like tracing the paths of some such objects and these days it's quite difficult to keep such things under the radar. If a particularly good item doesn't sell at auction it is often tainted with a 'no one wants me, there must be something wrong' stigma, particularly at the higher end of the market, and in the case of paintings it can be quite detrimental for them to go unsold in high-profile sales. However, this is not always the case. For this reason, I was attracted to an ivory and bronze figure by the famous Romanian sculptor Demetre Chiparus, pictured on the front of the *Antiques Trade Gazette*, a superb and rare tour de force in the world of Art Deco Chryselephantine figures and standing at an impressive 2ft 2in high. The figure had been unsold in a previous Bonhams sale in 2014. On that occasion it was estimated at £100,000–150,000 – not outside the realms of possibility considering Christie's in New York had sold another figure in 2008 for a sum equating to around £120,000.

As the *ATG* emphasised in their article, the ivory ban in the United States has certainly affected the market for items like this, yet when Bonhams re-offered it in their more recent sale it was estimated at a much-reduced £60,000–80,000, only to bring a show-stopping final result of £145,000! Although it was obviously not destined for the States, the market may be heartened to see it having done well amid the increasingly depressed feelings surrounding the commercial future of antique and collectable ivory-related artefacts.

Gottle o' Geer

The general impression of our ancestors is that they had absolutely no idea about the nutritional and health-related benefits of food. This simply isn't true. Victorians on the whole ate very healthy diets compared to our modern foods, living on diets of seasonal vegetables, fruit, plenty of offal, fish, nuts and seeds. In fact, Victorians apparently ate more calories than we do, and much larger amounts of food too, yet were still healthier, with instances of heart disease, diabetes and cancer at only 10 per cent of our modern rates. Yet, their scientific knowledge of vitamins and nutrition was limited and the evolution of this knowledge was largely delayed until well into the 20th century.

For some time, scientists had been able to isolate certain conditions as being diet-related – scurvy and rickets, for instance. We are all familiar with maritime tales of scurvy – caused by lack of vitamin C – which was rife among the ranks of sailors. Early attempts to ease the problem included ships taking on board limes or lemons and concentrates (that's where the term 'Limey' – meaning a Brit – comes from), but the way that vitamin C is degraded is strangely contradictory, or at least it was in past centuries, as no one understood that copper oxidises it and light degrades it too, meaning that concentrated lime juices that were prepared using copper piping and were then badly stored had virtually no vitamin C content whatsoever. Fresh lemons were the richest source. Some meats, such as seal and horse, also have higher levels of vitamin C, yet these contradictions could not easily be reconciled within the scientific parameters of the time and scurvy was still common.

The planning of many famous expeditions had to deal with the prospect of such outbreaks by making dietary plans that would help to thwart it. Most of this was trial and error and in James Cook's circumnavigation of the world (1768–71) the crew were fed sauerkraut and wort of malt – the liquid extracted from the mashing process during brewing! No crew member was lost to scurvy. Even Captain Scott, in his first expedition to the Antarctic in 1901, knew that scurvy was a serious problem but knowledge was still not sufficiently good to know how to stop it. However, his men ate plenty of seal meat, which thwarted any scurvy outbreaks from becoming fatal.

In 'Poles Apart II' (*see page 101*), I wrote about the ill-fated Franklin Expedition of 1845–48. A subsequent search for the missing party in 1851, commanded by Sir Edward Belcher, was equipped with a specially brewed beer called 'Arctic Ale'. It was thought to be an aid to preventing scurvy. Apparently two bottles survive from the expedition. The ale, made by Allsopp's, was again brewed in 1857 for a subsequent search mission. This time the voyage was commanded by Sir Leopold McClintock. Alas, no bottles are thought to have survived from this attempt. It was brewed yet again in 1875 for use on Sir George Nares' expedition to discover the North Pole – some bottles do survive from this journey. Nares was unsuccessful in his attempt.

Although a bottle had been sold in 2004 for £1,200, the discovery of another in a garage in Shropshire by auctioneers Trevanion & Dean was a rare find. The capsule is embossed 'Arctic Ale 1875' and although the auction house plumped on the conservative side with an estimate of £400–600, it surpassed this to make a vitamin-enriched hammer price of £3,300!

Reel Time

A fair amount of my childhood was characterised by balmy afternoons in the school summer holidays, carp fishing in the water-filled Second World War bomb craters that pockmarked the fields to the south of Coventry. The necessary equipment was pretty rudimentary: a basic fibreglass rod, a cheap reel, various accessories purchased at the local Woolworths and our secret weapon – sweetcorn. In fact, I once landed a carp weighing several pounds on an old stick, a piece of line and a hook; again, it was sweetcorn that did the trick! So, not being overly concerned with the more technical aspects of fishing, it wasn't until my days as an auctioneer that I really started to sit up and take notice of all the collectable paraphernalia that surrounds the sport.

The Cascapédia river (also known as the Grand Cascapédia) in the Gaspé Peninsula of Quebec, is a renowned Atlantic salmon river and is protected for almost the entirety of its 75-mile length. The lack of agriculture and development along its course means that the purity of the water is excellent, with no man-made pollutants affecting its carbonate-rich composition. By all accounts, the average catch for a salmon is around 20lbs. In 1886 a monster 54-pounder was caught and this record has yet to be beaten.

Unsurprisingly, the Cascapédia name has adorned many a fly reel made by the famous makers, Hardy. However, original examples from the 1930s are rare with only around a hundred or so made between 1931 and 1939. The earliest models had side plates made of Ebonite; this was then superseded by Duralum, an aluminium–copper alloy, which 'age-hardens'. (It was used in Zeppelins and early aircraft.) Mullock's auctioneers in Church Stretton were lucky enough to be able to offer one of these rarities in one of their specialist fishing sales. It even came in its original bag with the embroidered Hardy logo. Well priced at £9,000–10,000, the auctioneers had judged the market well as it realised a very healthy £12,000.

Barbarian Hordes

I'm familiar with a few Japanese characters – mainly those that I'm used to seeing on ceramics and bronzes. However, there is one term I know that is historically interesting and it's the word *Nanban*. Basically, the term, in Japanese has two characters:

$$南蛮$$

The first means 'south' or 'southern', the second means 'unrefined'; apparently, the word dates from the 14th century and was generally used to refer to foreigners, or, with the addition of other characters, objects emanating from foreign climes. Originally it referred to other Asians, perhaps from the Philippines or Indonesia, but following the arrival of the Portuguese in 1543 it was in common usage as a term to describe Europeans – with various connotations, such as 'southern barbarians' and 'wild red-haired barbarians'. This particularly applied to the Portuguese and Dutch, although the Dutch arrived later (c. 1600) and were referred to as *kōmō*, literally meaning 'red hair'.

So, in the art and antiques trade it's common to refer to Japanese items depicting Westerners as 'Nanban', as in the case of an exceptional 17th-century painted and gilded six-fold paper Nanban screen that was recently offered by

Christie's in their aptly named 'European Courts Encounter Japan' sale. Apparently there are just less than a hundred such examples surviving. This one features a beautiful and intricately executed scene of the arrival of a Portuguese trade ship. It had formerly belonged to the famous Japanese collector, dealer and connoisseur, Sakamoto Gorō. It sold for a commission-inclusive £818,500.

⁂

Woodn't it be Nice

Some years ago I purchased a very elegant Chinese rosewood altar table. Its pure simplicity and refined aesthetic makes it a joy to own, a stand-alone item that needs little more than a single Sang de Boeuf vase centrally placed on a carved hardwood stand. Imagine then, as over the intervening years, I have watched the value of such items rise at an incredible rate with similar examples making in excess of £100,000 at auction and provincial salerooms too turning up examples that have marched on from their low estimates to make £20,000. The difference is that the big money revolves around the actual, type of wood that they are fashioned from. The name for it is Huanghuali.

Huanghuali is a 'fragrant rosewood' of the genus

Dalbergia, a dense, slow-growing wood with a high oil content, which makes it very resistant to moisture; it ranges in hue from rich yellows to dark red and has a characteristically beautiful grain. It is an increasingly rare tropical hardwood that has been historically overexploited and is currently classified as vulnerable. It was revered in imperial times and utilised for objects and furniture used by the Emperor, his court and high ranking officials and scholars. In the Ming period the design of such furniture reached its zenith and pieces from this period are highly coveted by collectors. However, the demand for Huanghuali is also medicinal and there is a continued demand for the wood, meaning that the theft of Huanghuali from old buildings and temple sites is rife.

For the new breed of Eastern connoisseur collector, Huanghuali items have become an essential genre in a market that is pretty finite. Some experts put the actual amount of antique Huanghuali pieces at as few as 10,000. This was reflected in a recent offering by Bonhams where a low games table made from this exotic wood, with a central storage well, romped past its guide price of £8,000–12,000 to make £125,000. Alas, my lovely altar table is a less rare species!

Scraps of Knowledge

I've bought a lot of books this year. My favourite oddity is by Don Lemon – not the sort of name you'd expect as the author of a 19th-century book of facts and trivia; more an American-sounding moniker for a 1950s film star – but I couldn't resist the little book by this author entitled *Everybody's Scrap Book of Curious Facts*. Published in 1890 by Saxon & Co. in London, like the *Almanac*, it's a collection of curious articles on an incredibly diverse range of subjects. I like Don's preface. His idea that 'the paragraphs must not be too long', that 'it may contain much of suggestive value to everyone' and that it is 'a book for odd moments for busy people', rather encapsulates the idea behind *Allum's Antiques Almanac*.

So my rather ratty edition of Don's musings, complete with advertisements for Beecham's Pills and The Lightning Geyser Instant Hot Water Boiler, promised much in the way of inspiration. I was not disappointed – other than on the grounds that I would have preferred more material actually related to art and antiques; but there is much of a historical nature to be gleaned. I liked numerous little nuggets like 'At the last census there were sixteen gold pen factories in the United States, and they employed 254 hands, producing £96,000 worth of goods'. I was also highly amused by several annotations in pencil which indicate that the book's previous owner, a Mr G. Underwood according to the name in the front, had also been amused by various articles relating to the fairer sex. One such piece, with heavy underlining and entitled 'A Perfect Woman Nobly Planned', explained the perfect attributes for a female, including a bust 'from 28 to 36 inches' with hips measuring '6 to 10 inches more than this' and a waist calling for a belt from '22 to 28 inches'. Fascinating.

Other interesting statistics include the cost in human life of the wars fought in the previous 34 years – '2,553,000 souls', apparently, not including mortality from sickness (which would probably have accounted for the same number again).

Another nugget that grabbed my attention was itself about nuggets – gold nuggets. Here I decided to test out how accurate Don's 19th-century information was by cross-referencing some of the 'facts' with our thoroughly modern internet. 'Big Gold Nuggets' lists fourteen of the world's biggest finds, with Don carefully listing weights, find sites and prices paid for the gold at the time. Some of them are huge. Of the fourteen, seven were found at Ballarat, an area and later a city in the state of Victoria, Australia. Gold was discovered there in 1851 and a rush subsequently ensued, no doubt inspired by the discovery of several large nuggets. However, in 1872 the biggest specimen was found in Hill End, New South Wales. Called the

Haltman Nugget, according to Don, it weighed in at an incredible 640lbs and was judged to be worth £29,600. It was 4ft 9in high! Having done a little investigation through various sources it turns out that the nugget was in fact a veined matrix weighing 630lbs and containing 5,000 oz of gold. According to a Wikipedia entry which lists the New South Wales State Library among its various sources, a larger find was made but was broken up before it could be photographed. Interestingly, Don got the spelling wrong as the nugget is actually called the Holtermann Nugget, after Bernhardt Holtermann, a partner in the Star of Hope Gold Mining Company and later an invaluable benefactor in the photographic recording of Australia's early mining business. Most sources also put the value of the nugget at £10,000–12,000 – somewhat lower than the figure reported by Don. No doubt news was less accurately conveyed in the 19th century?

Anyway, differing information apart, I nosed around a little more and found that in 2013, interest in the Ballarat fields had been greatly revived by the discovery of a twelve-pound gold nugget worth an estimated $300,000 (US) – maybe up to $500,000 as a rare specimen. It was found by a prospector using a metal detector, not like my £120 version but one costing several thousand. It seems that's how a lot of gold prospecting is done these days – for nuggets, that is.

Bernhardt Otto Holtermann with the Holtermann Nugget.

Feeling Less Constable

You don't have to pay millions to own a work by John Constable. In 2014, a group of previously unknown drawings by Constable were offered by Cheffins of Cambridge. Found in a house in Norfolk, the seven sketches, along with another by his son Lionel, had apparently been purchased in the 1950s for £500 and had then languished until discovered by Cheffins. It's thought that they were perhaps made on his honeymoon. Pre-sale estimates were along the 'come get me' lines and interest was very strong prior to the sale but one thing these drawings allowed was the possibility that people from more ordinary walks of life might be able to buy into one of the country's most famous artists. Alas, the estimates were heavily surpassed, with a 'Picture of Storm Clouds' possibly near East Bergholt making £44,000 and a heavy horse and cart making £42,000 – the former was estimated at £6,000–8,000. In total the drawings made £187,000 – a good result for the vendor but possibly a bit out of the price range of most have-a-go collectors.

More recently, another drawing appeared at Mallams in Oxford. The pencil sketch of a head and shoulders from behind was a study of Constable's wife, Maria. It had been found in a house in Oxfordshire and was written up in Graham Reynolds' 1984 book *The Later Paintings and Drawings of John Constable* as 'whereabouts unknown'. Obviously, its reappearance caused some interest. Again it had been purchased in the 1950s or 60s. The estimate of £3,500–4,000 was again rather tempting and it surpassed that to make a fairly affordable £13,000.

Sèvres You Right

Marks on ceramics can be a nightmare. A little bit of knowledge can be a dangerous thing and in the case of the Sèvres factory it's easy to misinterpret the marks as those that appear on the wares of its many imitators, or as the marks of Sèvres' forerunner, the Vincennes factory. In this respect it is not unheard of for a piece of rare Vincennes to be catalogued as Sèvres, given that the marks look incredibly similar; this is where an expert knowledge of date letters and painters' marks, as well as patterns and styles is required – the preserve of the well-versed Continental ceramics specialist. This is also the case with other factories such as Meissen.

So I was not surprised to see reported in the trade press that Peter Wilson of Nantwich had catalogued a Vincennes sucrier as Sèvres in one of their auctions. The Vincennes factory was founded in 1740 and housed in the unused royal Château Vincennes. The Chinese formula for hard-paste porcelain had by this time become common knowledge and the Meissen factory was manufacturing it sourcing their own deposits of kaolin, an essential ingredient in the 'recipe'. The French factory had no kaolin and concentrated on a plan to make soft-paste porcelain, which did not initially go smoothly. It took five years for the factory to find its feet, with successive refinancing and eventually with support under the 'privilege' of Louis XV – granted in 1745. The use of famous sculptors and craftsmen from other disciplines gave the factory an impressively diverse and decorative output – not least in the style of 'wares from Saxony' (namely Meissen), as well as the French Rococo style. The use of vibrant deep colours such as *bleu lapis* that were decorative and richly gilded became a distinct trademark. However, in 1756 the operation moved to Sèvres and amid financial troubles it was purchased in its entirety in 1759 by the king and became the factory that most people instantly associate with the distinctive mark – Sèvres porcelain.

The small lidded sugar basin offered at Peter Wilson featured opposing vignettes of cherubs in a blue palette (*camaïeu bleu*) after Boucher; they were set on an overall yellow ground with gilded borders. The 'double Louis' mark dated the piece to 1753 and the painter's mark was for Vielliard. Vincennes pieces on yellow ground are exceptionally rare and given that fairly standard blue ground tankards and teapots from the factory can cost several thousand, this was destined to do well. The estimate, standing at £150–250, was never realistic but given that it was well advertised and on the internet, the pre-sale interest obviously meant that it had attracted the right buyers. Some might argue, given that it made £45,000 on the fall of the hammer, that it did better as a result. Hopefully everyone was happy.

Liar Liar

Apparently, it's a bit of a trait among sportsmen to exaggerate. We all know how difficult it is to gauge the size of a fish ('It was this big …') – I've probably done it myself. However, the practice of exaggerating the amount of game that was shot became quite a contentious issue in the Victorian period when personal 'bags' were often quoted in the newspapers. Norfolk, being the county of choice for many serious Victorian shooters, therefore spawned the 'Norfolk liar', a mechanical game counter that generally comprised two or three ratcheted counters that could be clicked to record the amount of game shot. (Of course, someone wishing to inflate their ego could click it as many times as they liked …) You can still buy a modern equivalent and they are still called Norfolk liars but I was interested to see a very nice 19th-century example, the dials set into the bone-veneered sides of a penknife made by Watson Brothers of Pall Mall, who are still in business as gun makers. This one, with three dials for 'Feathers' and two dials for 'Fur', was sold by Cheffins and made a pretty truthful £1,600!

War Torn

It's hard to imagine how some items end up where they do, yet objects continue to surface thousands of miles away from their original homes. However, this is no obstacle for collectors – the world has become a much smaller place – and both facts were apparent when a flag appeared at George Kidner Auctioneers in Dorset featuring a bald eagle grasping a bunch of arrows, surmounted by thirteen stars. Now, as most people know, this can only signify one thing – America. The flag, at just over 2ft square, was hand-painted on blue silk and fringed with braid. Although the condition was poor – a situation apparently caused by the propensity of flag-makers to soak the fabric in caustic mineral salts to give it more weight and increase its rigidity – it was obviously going to prove more interesting than the £100–150 estimate that had been placed on it. Dating from the American Civil War period but without the markings of a particular unit, it sold to an American buyer on the telephone for £2,800. I can't help feeling that he had a bit of a bargain. However, things are often worth more whence they came.

High Calibre

Elsewhere in this book I have written about sale of two handguns recovered from the scene of the fatal ambush that accounted for the lives of the famous criminals Bonnie and Clyde (*see* 'Gangster Rap', *page 173*). As you might expect, the market for such macabre artefacts is quite strong, particularly in America where guns, outlaws and gangsters seem to go hand-in-hand with the country's early history. Other famous firearms related to famous and infamous people have come up for sale on many occasions.

Annie Oakley, sharpshooter and star of *Buffalo Bill's Wild West Show*, defies the image of the usual stereotypical bank robber or outlaw, and was a sensation throughout her life as a star performer and extraordinary shot who, using her .22 calibre rifle, could split playing cards edge-on when thrown into the air – at a distance of 90 feet! Her 16 gauge Parker Brothers hammer gun sold for $293,000 in 2013.

Among other high-end guns sold in recent years was President Theodore Roosevelt's A.H. Fox 12 gauge shotgun. It may well be the one that he took on the 1909 Smithsonian-Roosevelt Expedition on which 11,400 specimens were collected for the Smithsonian's new Natural History Museum. It was this expedition that cemented his reputation as a prolific killer of big game but, without getting into the rights and wrongs of killing at all, it should be noted that in this respect the more pertinent figure is 512 animals and birds killed by Roosevelt and his companions; the rest of the specimens were either botanical or were smaller animal species such as bats and rodents. The shotgun sold for $862,500.

In 2011, Christie's in London offered the .38 calibre Colt of the famous Chicago mobster Al Capone at public auction. It was provenanced in writing by Capone's sister-in-law and sold for £67,250.

In 2003, the Smith & Wesson used by Bob Ford to murder the outlaw Jesse James sold for $350,000, while in 2013 another gun – a Colt Single Action Army .45 that actually belonged to Jesse James – was offered at Heritage Auctions and failed to sell on a $400,000 estimate. It is apparently valued at over $1.5 million but a valuation can be a different animal when people decide what they do or don't want to pay on the day!

I previously mentioned *Buffalo Bill's Wild West Show*; William Cody, aka Buffalo Bill, another famous, colourful Wild West character, led a varied life, riding for the Pony Express mail service, fighting in the Civil War with a Jayhawker unit, a guerrilla-type group, out of Kansas; and he even owned a hotel. He also worked as a Union scout and shot buffalo to feed the workers of the Transcontinental Railroad, reputedly shooting some 4,000 animals in eighteen months – hence his nickname. Between 1868 and 1872 he served as a civilian scout during the 'Indian Wars' and won a Congressional Medal for Bravery (it was later revoked because he was not serving in the military; the family refused to give it back and it was officially re-awarded in 1989). His gun from this period, an ivory-handled .44 calibre Remington was sold by Heritage Auctions in 2012. It made $239,000 and came with a card written by Cody that had been given with the gun when he gifted it to his good friends Charlie and Cary Trego – along with fourteen other letters to them. It was described by Heritage as the 'most important ... Cody gun extant'. In 2014, another of Cody's guns, a Colt .45, was also sold by Heritage and made $40,000. Interestingly enough, a bear-claw necklace worn by Cody made an identical amount in the same sale.

Most recent were several pieces related to legendary gambler, lawman, miner and pimp Wyatt Earp. Famous for his part in the shootout at the O.K. Corral, Earp is synonymous with the folklore of the Wild West and is also one of American history's most infamous gunslingers. His Colt .45, which was supposedly used at the O.K. Corral, was offered by auctioneers J. Levine in Scottsdale, Arizona where it realised $225,000. Gruesome I know, but a source of eternal fascination to those interested in the history of the American West.

N.B. During the course of researching this piece I came across what I thought was a pretty amazing little museum

William Cody, aka Buffalo Bill.

— one that perhaps could only happen in America. It's called the Cody Dug Up Gun Museum. It's in Cody, Wyoming — the town founded by Buffalo Bill — and it does exactly what it says on the label. Essentially, it's full of hundreds of dug-up 'relic' guns dating from all periods of American history. Looking at the pictures online (www. codydugupgunmuseum.com), it features many weapons, including Civil War examples lost in the heat of battle — some still loaded! Apparently it's free.

Grave Thought

Following on from the previous piece, I recently read an article in *The Sunday Times* concerning the whereabouts of Bill Cody's mortal remains. By the time of his death in 1917, he had retired to Cody, Wyoming (as mentioned above, the town that he founded). However, he passed away when visiting his sister in Colorado and was buried on Lookout Mountain, Golden, in that state. His grave can be seen at The Buffalo Bill Museum & Grave. However, there is an ongoing controversy about whether the body buried there is actually his. This came about because his original will stated that he wished to be interred in Cody, although this was later superseded with no location stipulated for his burial place. Amid stories of a mortuary-room snatch and body substitution, his niece later said that he needed to be moved, and a group also apparently offered $10,000 in the 1940s to anyone who would dig him up and return him to Cody. This resulted in an 11ft-thick concrete slab being put over the grave and a guard being posted. The forthcoming centenary of his death in 2017 has naturally raised the stakes – the gravesite is a big tourist revenue generator – and by all accounts, the Republican governor of Wyoming, Matt Mead, and his Democrat 'oppo' John Hickenlooper in Colorado will be meeting to discuss the issue. I'll update you in the next *Almanac*!

Drink Up

Some objects are so rare that their appearance on the market can be quite easily tracked over successive decades. Watching them reappear is always an interesting exercise in studying the worth and strength of both the objects themselves and the buoyancy of the markets, yet such rarity can often be the domain of entrepreneurial top-flight dealers who corner the market in various genres and consequently influence the value while supplying the best collectors.

I've had a few friends over the decades who have judged it right, or sometimes wrong, making hay while the economic sunshine of certain economies filled their pockets but not quite anticipating the right time to opt out. The antiques market has always been a difficult one to second-guess.

English ceramics are an interesting area. The auction world constantly moans about the lack of interest in English china but as with all genres, it's the best of any area that wins out. There have been some big players over the years – eminent dealers and collectors such as Jonathan Horne were the 'go-to' people for the best of English Delft and early English pieces. Prime examples of dated Delft 17th- and 18th-century royal portrait wares continue to represent the top of the tree; indeed, anything rare and royal will excite the serious collector.

One such object was a pottery 'wine bottle' with a blue and white 'C★R' cipher under a crown for Charles I and on a manganese coloured ground. One of only two known, it was sold in 2004 by Bonhams, again in 2008 for £70,000 as part of the Simon Sainsbury collection (of supermarket fame), and when re-offered this year at the Christie's 'Centuries of Style' sale it made £78,000. It seems to me that when you take into consideration the commissions involved, the only people who made any money on the last two deals were Christie's … although it did largely hold its value. Interestingly, another not dissimilar pottery wine bottle was sold by Bonhams in 2007 and although less striking in terms of the depth of the manganese colour, it bore the cipher of Queen Henrietta Maria, wife of Charles I. It was previously unrecorded and made a premium-inclusive £60,000.

Take That

I frequently lend a hand as a charity auctioneer. Over the years I've been lucky enough to sit at many a top table with various celebrities and even the odd royal. It's been great fun and has taken me to many glamorous venues, with the best reward of all being the opportunity to help make a difference when some humorously coercive bids help raise more money for good causes. So it's always good to see those who can help giving their time and possessions to raise much-needed cash and one such occasion this year was the 'Doing it for the Kids' Robbie Williams charity sale in which 159 lots were donated by Robbie for the benefit of the Donna Louise Children's Hospice, of which Robbie is a patron.

There were plenty of Take That items as well as personal clothing, awards, photographs and ephemera – everything for the die-hard Take That and Robbie Williams fan. Highlights from the sale included £10,625 for an MTV music award in the form of a spaceman and a massive £31,250 for the handwritten lyrics of 'Go Gentle' (including commission). The overall result for the charity was a very helpful £150,000.

✳❀❧❀✳

Design for Life

£2.1 million is a lot of money for a piece of furniture. It might be conceivable if it were a Chippendale masterpiece or a bejewelled 16th-century cabinet of curiosities but the one I'm thinking of is neither. The piece in question is a modern aluminium and fibreglass chaise by the Australian designer Marc Newson, a clever reinvention of the 'lounger' which owes much to the form and construction of aircraft.

Newson has become an iconic and influential designer. He was born in 1963 and graduated from the Sydney College of the Arts in 1984. His first exhibition featured the aforementioned chaise – a curvaceous aluminium welded and riveted construction on a fibreglass frame, named the Lockheed Lounge in a nod to the American aircraft company Lockheed. It has recently become the most expensive piece of furniture by a living designer ever to sell at auction – sold by Phillips – and would have cost the anonymous buyer some £2,434,500 including commission. The prototype for this chaise was previously sold (also by Phillips) for £1.4 million in 2010 and was the previous record holder for a living designer. The Lockheed was made famous by its appearance in the 1993 Madonna video for the track 'Rain'.

There are fifteen Lockheed Lounges in existence. Ten were made as a limited edition; there were four artist proofs and the original prototype. You might ask why people are prepared to pay so much money for what is quite an uncomfortable piece of furniture? Obviously, it's more complicated than this. Groundbreaking designs influence the world around them, and the Lockheed is a classic, highly recognisable and seminal piece of imaginative design. It already has its place in the design hall of fame, as does Marc Newson himself, alongside other great design protagonists of the 20th century. Newson, though, is a designer for the 21st century too, and the Lockheed can be seen as foreshadowing this progression. He currently works with Apple but has operated in many areas including clothing, jewellery and product design.

And just in case you are wondering how much a Lockheed would have originally cost – it was US$1,000!

What the Dickens

Philanthropists and benefactors are often essential to the large legacies and trusts that help to support major institutions such as hospitals. Great Ormond Street Children's Hospital in London, founded in 1852, has been the beneficiary of many such bequests and generous donations, most famously that of J.M. Barrie's copyright to Peter Pan, in 1929, which has provided significant funding for the famous hospital. It also has other strong literary associations: Charles Dickens was an early fundraiser and close friend of the chief physician Dr Charles West.

The desk and chair at which Dickens sat to write classics such as *Great Expectations* had been handed down through his family and were owned by his great-great-grandson Christopher Charles Dickens. After his death in 1999, they were donated to the Great Ormond Street Charitable Trust by his widow Jeanne-Marie Dickens, Countess Wenckheim. In 2008 Christie's offered them for sale with an estimate of £50,000–80,000. The desk can clearly be seen in the picture *Dickens' Dream* by R.W. Buss and in an 'in memoriam' engraving by the artist Sir Luke Fildes, which shows the empty chair and desk in the author's study. Mounted with an engraved plaque, the importance of the duo in literary history was always going to be difficult to evaluate but the estimate was easily surpassed to reach an inclusive £433,250.

However, that's not the end of the story as recently the desk and chair came into the news again with the headlines that the National Heritage Memorial Fund had made a donation of £780,000 to acquire the desk and chair for the Dickens Museum at 48 Doughty Street in London, the author's home for two years between 1837 and 1839 – a considerable amount more than the 2009 price! The desk and chair had actually come from his last home, Gad's Hill in Kent, and the design, with its central rising writing surface, is of a kind that is now commonly called a 'Dickens Desk'.

Attic Find

I'm often intrigued by the labels in museums that attribute the painting on Greek vases to certain artists. How, you might think, is this achieved?

Many of the names – and there are over 2,000 attributed painters – are designated with monikers such as 'Kiss Painter', 'Pig Painter', 'Flying Angel Painter', 'Thanatos Painter', 'Daybreak Painter', 'Orpheus Painter' and so on. The periods are generally split into the Geometric Period, Orientalising Period, Black Figure Period, Red Figure Archaic Period (considered one of the most important forms of Greek vase painting) and Red Figure Classical Period.

Establishing the identities of vase painters is a long academic tradition. Pioneers included Sir John Davidson Beazley (1885–1970) who by intensive research and the application of 'the art-historical method' was able to attribute the different hands of workshops and specific painters. It was Beazley who first identified the 'Berlin Painter', named after an amphora in the Antikensammlung, Berlin. None of the painter's works are signed but they are nevertheless distinctive with their red figures on glossy black backgrounds. He also produced a series of red figure vases. Strangely, most of his work has been found in Italy, used as lavish grave goods in the necropoli of southern coastal Italy and Tuscany and Umbria, areas of heavy Greek settlement and of course home to the Etruscans.

Without the painstaking and comparative work of people like Beazley there would be no reliable list of Greek painters. So the next time you are in a museum spare a thought for the decades and decades of study that went into the attribution on the label.

What about owning one? In reality, £5,000–10,000 will buy you a 5th-century BC Bell Krater with an attributed painter and a watertight provenance and there have been many on the market in various auctions. However, one of my favourites was a lovely Column Krater, a 5th-century BC beauty depicting Heracles (Hercules) and another warrior, each fighting an Amazon. Attributed to the Group of Faina, it was sold by Sotheby's in New York for $81,250.

Persian Perfection

Reading good catalogue descriptions is a joy. Some are so finely researched and academically supported that their very compilation acts as part of the historical record of the object itself. Manuscripts are a case in point. Unravelling some of the descriptions also often leads to a far greater contextual interest in the history of previous owners, the place of the object in history and its association with other similar artefacts. All in all, what initially appears to be a five-minute job can spin off into an hour of antiquarian Chinese whispers, as one thing leads to another and my overlapping Google tabs become so small you can hardly see them.

Such was the case when I started following up the news and results for Sotheby's 'Arts of the Islamic World' auction – and I should make clear that what is written here bears little correlation to the time I have spent filling my brain with even more amazing material. Initially, my interest was fired by the results of some Qur'an leaves; firstly, a rather scrappy-looking page, some 33cm × 22cm, which was catalogued by Sotheby's as:

> An early Qur'an leaf in Hijazi script on vellum, Arabian Peninsula, second half 7th century AD.

This leaf is not only considered to be a part of one of the earliest group of Qur'an manuscripts in existence but also one of the earliest examples of Arabic script. In short, it is of great rarity and an incredible text in that it was written not long after the death of the prophet Muhammad in AD632. It made £245,000.

Another Qur'an page with gold 'stretched' Kufic script on a striking blue-dyed vellum background and dating from the 9th–10th century, is from a Qur'an simply known as the 'Blue Qur'an' and noted as 'one of the most luxurious manuscripts produced in the early medieval period in the Islamic world'. Other parts of this distinctive work are housed in the National Institute of Art and Archaeology in Tunis and various other collections both private and public including the Museum of Fine Arts, Boston and the Harvard University Art Museums. Other pages have also been sold in the past, including another offered by Sotheby's in 2011, which sold for £277,250, and one sold by Christie's in 2012 for £241,250. This latest offering sold for £365,000, a good £100,000 more than the others.

However, the tour de force of such manuscripts must surely be the page offered in the same sale that sold for £389,000. Described by Sotheby's as 'one of the most beautiful and striking Qur'anic scripts', this page is a rare survivor from a work executed between AD1075 and 1125, probably in Persia or Central Asia. Catalogued as 'one of the most luxurious Qur'ans of the medieval period' it is one page of a probable 2,250 pages produced in 30 volumes. Three sections survive and are in American collections. They were most likely acquired in the 1920s and 30s from the dealer and collector Kirkor Minassian who supplied many American institutions and collections with Eastern material. Staggeringly beautiful and almost beyond comprehension in terms of the work required to complete such a manuscript, it's little wonder that parts are so valuable, although when multiplied up on the basis of £389,000 per page, the complete 30 volumes would be worth somewhere in the region of £875,000 million. Crumbs!

Flat Weave

My house is populated by a collection of Persian carpets, largely purchased because I either liked the pattern or they were cheap. That's not to say that some of them aren't quite good, it's just that I have always been an opportunist buyer when it comes to covering my floors in decorative rugs and carpets. My favourite is one that belonged to J.B. Priestley. Several are flat weaves, that is, they are woven on looms rather than knotted and have a distinctive 'flat' and rather tough feel – they are known to most people as kelims (or kilims).

Now, I'm not a carpet expert and nor would I even suggest that I know any more than a few styles and distinctive types of rugs and carpets – it's a minefield and very complicated and better left to the specialists. However, I couldn't help noticing a 'flatwoven wool carpet', that was being offered in a Christie's sale as '13th or 14th-century

Mongol Empire' and mooted as perhaps the sole surviving example of its type. The pre-sale write-up justifying its age and design and citing comparative work from research on other textiles of the period was interesting for a carpet that appears to be a unique survivor. I investigated further on the internet and turned up some conspiracy theories about the supposed age and provenance of the carpet, or 'tapestry', as some preferred to call it.

It seems that the same carpet was advertised on a dealer's catalogue cover from Nepal in 1987; at that point it was apparently in the possession of a dealer who had allegedly supplied other textiles and carpets with dubious provenances. To be honest, I am unlikely to ever know the truth of it but the 'Mongol flatweave' still sold for an all-inclusive £602,500, not a small amount. Perhaps time will tell.

Mysore Magic

Better to die like a soldier than live a miserable
[life] dependent on the infidels ...
I would rather live two days as a
tiger than 200 years as a sheep.
—TIPU SULTAN, THE TIGER OF MYSORE (1750–1799)

I recently purchased a carved Indian alabaster figure of a tiger mauling a person. Highlighted with gilt, black and gold colouring, I bought it for one reason alone, its distinct similarity to the famous Tipu's Tiger, a wonderful automaton of a tiger eating a European, made for Tipu Sultan (1759–1799), the wonderfully defiant and proud Tiger of Mysore and French-allied arch enemy of the British and the British East India Company. Tipu was also fiercely expansionist and fought with his neighbouring states too but to many he is a hero. Tipu's Tiger can be seen in the Victoria & Albert Museum.

My little alabaster is likely nothing to do with Tipu. The beleaguered figure looks to be wearing Indian attire and, considering how many Indians have been killed and eaten by tigers, it's likely to be a folk-like depiction of a relatively common occurrence. However, if it were associated, it would no doubt be of considerable interest and this was definitely the case when Bonhams offered some 30 lots of items related to Tipu as part of Islamic Week in London.

As I've said on previous occasions, it's hard to judge what might happen when items come back on to the market relatively quickly and Bonhams were faced with no easy task in estimating objects that had been sold ten years earlier at Sotheby's major dispersal of the Tipu collection of Robin Wigington, arms and armour dealer, expert and collector of Tipu material. To be honest, I'm sure that he

The alabaster figure.

would have been astounded by some of the prices subsequently attained.

The Sultan was defeated and killed by the British after the siege of his capital, Seringapatam, a battle in which a young Arthur Wellesley, later the Duke of Wellington, was honing his skills as a general. Perhaps the most iconic lot in the sale was the jewelled sword from Tipu's treasury, a gem of an object, the hilt modelled with Tipu's defiant tiger motif. It sold in 2005 for £50,000. This year it sold for £1.85 million. A three-pounder bronze cannon from Seringapatam, which sold for £55,000 in 2005, made £1.2 million and a fabulous 18th-century flintlock sporting gun from Tipu's armoury, the butt carved with a trademark tiger, sold for £600,000 this year having realised £100,000 in 2005. Most of the items were purchased by Sir Ninian Mogan Lourdenadin, the Anglo-Malaysian businessman. No doubt business has been good with the ascent of the Asian Tiger (no pun intended) but when I see such dramatic rises in value in just ten years I can only speculate on the reasons for such a huge surge in price – right place, right time, I suppose. However, another sword had been offered in 2013 by Sotheby's in their 'Art of Imperial India' auction, a much plainer, utilitarian example comprising a captured English blade by Woolley & Deakin that had been remounted with a tiger-shaped hilt à la Tipu Sultan – a suitable act of defiance. It sold for £98,500.

So, it's something to bear in mind. Although the tiger is a common motif in Indian art, there's always the chance that it might be something to do with Tipu. Everything he had made featured an attribute associated with this majestic and sometimes ferocious creature.

Field Find

My metal detector rarely sees the light of day but being the owner of such a device gave me a sort of empathy with the characters of the wonderful BBC4 comedy-drama *The Detectorists*, in which the main characters, Lance and Andy, are a couple of 'nerdy' archeao-detectorists, convinced that they will find a major 'treasure' near the fictional town of Danebury. Although several of my friends just didn't seem to get it, I thought it was one of the best-observed comedy-dramas I had seen for years – God forbid I turn out like that!

Whether or not it has endeared the hobby to more people is debatable; it may even have upset ardent detectorists. However, there seems to have been no abatement in the level of good finds made with metal detectors and given that some major archaeological discoveries have been instigated as a result of these, it's good to see that when responsibly observed, the hobby can reap enormous benefits for both individuals and the archaeological community.

There are plenty of little gems that have come to auction. Found in a Somerset field and duly declared as Treasure Trove was a 16th-century St George Ring. Intricately 'chip-carved' with a representation of the saint, it was executed at a time when St George was replacing St Edmund as patron saint of England. It was offered by Greenslade Taylor Hunt with an estimate of £3,000–4,000 and even though misshapen, made a resplendent £7,000.

However, this single ring seems rather paltry compared to some other sizeable finds. Paul Coleman, a member of the Weekend Wanderers Metal Detecting Club, found 5,251 silver coins dating back to the Anglo-Saxon period in a field near Aylesbury. Then there was Derek McLennan who discovered one of the biggest and most varied Viking hoards yet unearthed. Consisting of over 100 items, including ingots, brooches and a silver alloy Carolingian vessel, it was discovered on Church of Scotland land in Dumfries and Galloway upon which he had permission to detect. This after McLennan had also recently found 322 medieval coins in a field near Twynholm – a significant find in its own right. The Viking hoard is the largest and most significant one of its kind to be found in Scotland since 1891 ... who's laughing now?

Devo-Max

I won't go into the politics – it's too contentious and divisive; suffice to say, I'm Scottish from my mother's side, proud to wear a kilt, my family motto is 'Stand Fast' and I think we're all better off in it together – right, now that's off my chest ...

Following the General Election and with many newly elected Scottish National Party MPs now in Westminster, perhaps it's no surprise that the patriotism that was evident at Lyon & Turnbull's 'Jacobite, Stuart and Scottish Applied Arts' auction in Edinburgh led to a 90 per cent success rate. To be honest, such well-connected lots have always raised the emotions of ardent Jacobite supporters. Then there's the rarity of some of the artefacts: a wonderful 'bullet-shaped' teapot, the cobalt blue ground decorated with a Jacobite rose and a 'C★R III' cipher for King Charles III – aka Bonnie Prince Charlie – is one of only two thought to exist. The manufacture of such pieces constituted a risk for the Staffordshire factories but no doubt commerce out-weighed politics and the few such pieces that were made are now rare. It sold for £8,000.

Key to such sales is provenance. Jacobite fakes abound; many items were revisited in the 19th century on the back of a very Victorian revival – particularly glass – so indisput-able history or source information is invaluable. Such was the case with a French gold-enamelled pocket watch beau-tifully decorated with the young pretender's cipher: a lion and unicorn, roses, thistles and an oak leaf signifying the tree in which Charles II hid after the battle of Worcester. Engraved for 'JQ, Elio Bircharch Paris' and dated 1758, it sold for £24,000.

Another lot which bore its identity in the form of an inscription was a late 17th-century blunderbuss by James Spencer of London. Dating from c. 1690, it had, according to the engraved explanation, been 'taken from a Highlander at Preston 1715 loaded with 17 balls'. Just in case you are wondering, that's the 'battle' or siege of Preston in Lancashire, usually known as the First Jacobite Rebellion. The Jacobites eventually surrendered after killing and wounding some 300 government troops, losing seventeen of their own men. Almost 2,000 Scottish and English Jacobites were taken prisoner. The blunderbuss sold for £21,000.

Long live the Union!

Happy Birthday

2015 is the 150th anniversary of the London jewellers Wartski. Geoffrey Munn OBE, one of my colleagues on the *Antiques Roadshow* and perhaps one of the most erudite and charming people that I have ever met, is the managing director. The firm was established by Morris Wartski, a Russian emigré who set up the business in Bangor in North Wales in 1865, specialising in Fabergé.

The company, now located at 14 Grafton Street, London W1, is owned by Nicholas Snowman, great-grandson of Morris Wartski, and holds Royal Warrants from the Queen and Prince Charles. It is beyond doubt one of the most amazing premises to visit and has a renowned reputation for its superlative stock of Fabergé and other historic and precious jewels.

Happy birthday Wartski!

✻

Lots of Bottle

I was a teenage bottle digger. Not exactly Hollywood material, but true nevertheless. I cut my collecting teeth on these freebies dug from bottle dumps and canal banks and was always in pursuit of such 'holy grail' examples as the 'Warner's Safe Cure' with its characteristic safe moulded on the side. (I have one.) Others were the cobalt versions of 'Codd' and 'Hamilton' bottles. If you're not au fait with some of these patent designs, the Hamilton, also known as a Torpedo bottle, is a distinctive bottle that won't stand up. In fact, it was designed – in 1814 – specifically so that it wouldn't stand up, by a man called William Hamilton. He was looking for a solution for storing carbonated water, which was prone to problems caused by cork stoppers in conventional bottles drying out, shrinking and leaving retailers with no gas in their water. The ovoid bottle meant that it had to be stored lying down, thus keeping the cork damp and swollen. The bottle became a standard in the Victorian period and I dug up many as a boy, but never a blue one – they are exceedingly rare and can make in excess of £1,000.

Over the last couple of years there have been some interesting variations on the Hamilton design, sold by BBR Auctions of Barnsley, South Yorkshire (specialists in this field). A 'flat-bottomed' example was sold in 2013 for £340; a Sturgeons Hamilton-type bottle for 'preserved milk' made £600; several salt-glazed stoneware versions with Calcutta addresses on them made around £500 each; and a silver-plated Hamilton bottle holder for the table, made by Elkington & Co., made £290 – it looked rather like a giant egg holder.

As for the Codd, this bottle is renowned as the source of many a marble. The design is clever and has even warranted its own Wikipedia entry. Designed in 1872/73 by Hiram Codd, the 'globe-stoppered' bottle was an ingenious alternative to unreliable corks and used a glass marble within a specially shaped chamber and a rubber gasket in the neck. It was filled upside down and the gas sealed the marble very tightly to the 'O' ring. Codd's enterprise was highly successful. Initially he sold licences to companies who wanted to use the patented design, but then he hatched a system whereby he gave the licence free on the understanding that the licensee purchased the marbles, the sealing rings and the special tool that was needed to make the seating within the neck from his company. Codd, along with his partners, was very successful and the many small boys that smashed open the bottles in order to recover the marbles were no doubt very grateful too! Again, I dug up many and had several nice ones in my collection, including various permutations on his patent such as the 'Niagara', with four dimples in the neck. There are by all accounts some 100 variations on the original Codd patent, one of the more unusual being the 'egg-ended hybrid' – a cross between a Codd and a Hamilton. I was of course always after another variation for my childhood collection, with the 'grail' blue one at the top of my wish list. In 2008 a Stewart's Hartlepool blue Codd made a staggering £7,700 at BBR Auctions. More recently, a hybrid was sold for £1,300, also by BBR.

The Japanese have been drinking a brand of soft drink called Ramune since 1841. It's still sold in a version of the Codd bottle – a nice historical throwback. The bottles are recycled – a practice of which Hiram Codd would have approved, as he himself introduced a bottle recycling system in 1880.

Just One Drink

Tintin is perhaps one of the world's most famous comic book characters. He was created in 1929 by the Belgian cartoonist Georges Prosper Remi, better known by his pen name of Hergé. Tintin, together with his dog Snowy, is a clever and adventurous teenager whose ability to solve mysteries and escape from all sorts of dangerous situations has been an enduring attraction to young boys (and adults) such as myself for the last 85 years. I suppose one of the main attractions is that Tintin really knows how to handle himself, which makes him just as happy with a machine gun as with a pen ... of course, there have been criticisms levelled at his character, particularly issues related to race; however, his behaviour and character traits were written within the context of different periods and changing ideologies, which make him historically reliant for some of his quirks. Whatever your views, he still continues to delight millions of people and the market for Tintin collectables is always hot.

Foremost on the list are original works by Hergé. In 2012 the original artwork for the cover of *Tintin in America* was sold for €1.3 million – at the time a world record for a comic. Dating from 1932, it had previously been sold in 2008 for €764,218 – a good rise in just four years. More recent high-fliers include the 2014 result of €289,500 paid at Christie's for a page of sketches for *Tintin in Tibet*, dating from 1960. And, in this last year, the Christie's sale of just ten lots saw one original work by Hergé of the 1978 cover for *Le Journal de Tintin* realise €480,000 – more than half the value of the whole sale!

In reality there are very few original Tintin works left in the public domain but if you really are a fan and fancy a trip to Belgium then a visit to Musée Hergé (www.museeherge. com) is a must.

Slave Trader

You never know what you might turn up on a house valuation. On many occasions I've found very distasteful items, objects that challenge your sense of morality and good taste: illegal firearms, pornography, strange substances, dangerous objects and Nazi memorabilia – all having to be dealt with in a way that is either sympathetic to the issues involved or within the parameters of the law.

As a result of working in the 'history' business, I'm obviously no stranger to objects associated with the slave trade. Indeed, I have handled several 18th-century artefacts such as abolitionist lockets and related mementos. In fact, such items fascinate me and cannot truthfully be sidelined – nor should they be; after all, we cannot alter the course of history and neither should we endeavour to annul it. More important is how we handle such areas of historical disgrace and man's inhumanity to man.

So, imagine that on a day-to-day basis you might find yourself putting through your auctions items such as a 'Jolly Nigger Bank'. These commonly occurring cast iron (sometimes aluminium) money boxes were just one of a raft of derogatory items produced throughout the 19th century and well into the 20th in a shamefully arrogant and racially scurrilous and offensive way, portraying African-Americans as both negative stereotypes and targets of acceptable aggressive behaviour.

One day, in my early days of auctioneering, I came across a game dating from the early 20th century called 'Good Bye! Sambo', in which the colourfully printed lid depicted a black boy hanging from some branches over a crocodile-infested pool. The game included a cheap pressed tin gun and a card target board, which if hit in the right place by a wooden projectile would drop a small black boy into the jaws of a croc. Nice. My immediate reaction was to put it in the bin; that was until I started to research the wider context for such games. The fact is that this trade was rife in America and such games were routinely given to white children who, from the word go, were being fed a racially prejudiced doctrine. Even a quick browse through a British catalogue such as the 1913 Gamages Bazaar reveals several toys and games such as 'The Whistling Nigger' and 'Alabama Coon'. After some discussion we decided to enter it for auction and it made several hundred pounds. The buyer was an African-American.

Generally termed 'black memorabilia', it's estimated that over three-quarters of collectors of such items are African-Americans and include such famous personalities as Oprah Winfrey – her donation in 2013 of $12 million towards the Smithsonian Museum of Black American History made her one of its biggest single benefactors. Swann Auctioneers in New York now have an annual African-Americana sale and although some of the items that are offered are shocking to most people's sensibilities and morals, they are historically important. One such lot in their last sale was a copy of *The Negro Motorist Green Book*, a guide for black drivers that would help them, when travelling through the 'Old South' to find friendly service stations, restaurants and lodgings. Such was the continual lack of progress on civil rights that this book was published right up until the 1960s. It made $18,000. A cheaply produced printed broadside or advertising sheet that would have been pasted up to advertise a slave auction, dating from around 1848, sold for $30,000.

I have one item at home – a manilla. It's a penannular

copper bangle or armlet that was produced by Europeans for slavers as a tradeable commodity and upon which the value of human life was based. It's a highly emotive object.

⁂

Cable Tie

The history of transatlantic communication is fascinating – but I'm not talking here about snail mail; I'm interested in the story of early telegraphic communication and all the trials and tribulations that went into establishing a reliable transatlantic link. The reason it interests me so much is that on several occasions I have come across sections of cable, often nicely mounted or with engraved plaques explaining their origins – they are wonderful curios of woven copper, gutta-percha and steel. Recently, I was on a valuation and found two such pieces; only a few inches long each, they were prepared by hand in a stepped 'cut-back' cross-section showing the different layers of insulation and cable. Sadly, neither had a label but the idea that they formed part of an early communications system was enough for me to value them at a few hundred pounds. No doubt their construction can be cross-referenced with some other known sections.

The first cable linking America to Britain had been mooted in the 1840s. The Atlantic Telegraph Company was set up by an American businessman called Cyrus West Field, who along with other financiers and entrepreneurs enabled the laying of the first transatlantic cable in 1857–58. This huge undertaking was executed by two ships, the USS *Niagara* and HMS *Agamemnon*. The route was from Valentia Island in western Ireland to Heart's Content in Newfoundland. On the first attempt, the cable snapped after several hundred miles had been laid out and could not be recovered. On the second, the two ships successfully rendezvoused and the cables were spliced together. On 16 August 1858, the first official Morse code telegram was sent between Queen Victoria and President James Buchanan. It was triumph, but a short-lived one, as the cable started to deteriorate quickly and the transmission times declined rapidly so that a simple message would take many hours to transmit. Eventually, after just three weeks, the cable stopped working, a situation that was largely blamed on the American engineer Wildman Whitehouse who apparently 'fried' the cable by applying excessive voltage to it – in reality, it was a fragile cable and a fledgling technology and Whitehouse probably did little more than hasten the inevitable.

Leftover cable from the first attempt, which had been snapped up at the New York end, was cut into small sections which were then sold as souvenirs by Tiffany of New York for 50 cents apiece. Each section was accompanied by a facsimile letter from Cyrus West Field guaranteeing its authenticity, but enthusiasm for such items quickly dissipated as the cable failed. Over the decades there have been numerous reported discoveries in America of crates full of unsold sections, each sporting a little brass plaque from Tiffany – several thousand in all.

It was some time before a more reliable cable was laid, by Brunel's SS *Great Eastern*. The initial attempt in 1865 failed, with the cable having to be spliced through pay-out damage on more than one occasion and then breaking and being lost. Several attempts to recover it failed and it eventually had to be abandoned. It's a complicated story and a tale of great endurance and patience – not to mention huge monetary cost – but another cable was successfully laid in 1866, and the 1865 cable was also recovered. This prompted many more successful cables around the world and the speed of intercontinental communications was irrevocably changed.

A Tiffany souvenir piece will generally cost any would-be collector around £300–500. Small slices of the 1865 cable mounted as pendants cost a similar amount and are very hard to find.

EPILOGUE

'I wouldn't be a valuer for anything – it's an impossible job!' These words, still ringing in my ears, were from a conversation with a good friend that took place several months ago. I seem to remember that I was moaning. I'd attached some values to some objects for a client and consigned them to a saleroom, only to have the estimates heavily knocked back by the 'specialist' – embarrassing to say the least. Yet, I knew in my heart of hearts that my intuition was probably correct. Luckily, they went to sale, without being withdrawn by the vendor, where they made three times the revised estimate. Of course, it's highly satisfying to be vindicated in that way but perfectly illustrative of the complicated wrangles about 'value' that it's so easy to get embroiled in.

My friend was right – to a certain extent. Valuing objects can be a really difficult job. To be frank, there are lots of people in my industry that think it's a waste of time trying to decide what people are prepared to pay at all but that's a fine assertion when you are working against other auction houses who have given their own punchy estimates in a bid to gain the business, yet you are having to compete to assure your customer that what you are saying is to your mind correct. Then there are the awkward moments when a second opinion from a fellow expert is so different from your own valuation that it is impossible to reconcile the two, so you stick to your original estimate and wait for the flak ... ah, the joys of valuation.

Luckily, there are plenty of precedents for many types of items. Some are so out of fashion or undesirable that it's hardly possible to sell them at all; others draw you in like the mesmeric, hypnotic spiralling eyes of the Cheshire cat, their beauty and craftsmanship – or simply blatant big-bucks commercialism – a simple and obvious key to their latent potential. Sometimes it all seems like the most ridiculous game, yet it is still so utterly compelling because in reality it's like playing a colossal game of chess; every day you move a different piece and place it on another square, manoeuvring within a market that has lots of other very good players huddled around the board. It's a buzz and it's essential to think ahead. Keeping your opponents guessing is paramount; concealing your inner feelings can be key in the bustle of a busy auction house; surrounding the king doesn't always mean that you have won. Things can change in a moment and another year in the market place has added to that understanding. It's been busier than ever, probably more stressful too, but the rewards have been both personally fulfilling and hopefully helpful to others. As ever, I have continued to learn and I relish the idea that my terms of reference are shifted continually by new discoveries, market news, archaeological wonders and the people that I meet. I hope you enjoyed the selection in *Allum's Antiques Almanac 2016* as much as I enjoyed compiling it.

ACKNOWLEDGEMENTS

How do you measure success? Cash often helps; it's the most base indicator of what most people term 'success' and yet when I sat down with Icon Books and we talked about the vehicle that is *Allum's Antiques Almanac*, it was an honest punt at an area of the market that was – in this format – a little uncharted. Honestly, I didn't think about the money and I'm sure that my lovely publishers Icon knew that they were taking a chance on its success too. Projects like the *Almanac* are invariably a slow burn. It takes a while to build up a solid foundation for an annual publication and measuring the success after one volume is not necessarily an indicator of its longer-term prospects. However, it has been very well received – volumes have been shifted – and the consequence of this has been what I can only describe as a roller coaster of post-publication literary festival overload! I mean that in the best possible way, because if there's one thing that the circuit teaches you, it's the importance of connecting with your readership. I love being out on the road and enthusing about what I do through my passion for collecting and my love of storytelling. Sometimes I feel like an antiquarian mystic Sufi, trying to assert my divine interest in the world of objects through constant travels around the literary temples of middle England, preaching to each group of people eagerly awaiting conversion to the god of materialism, their mantelpieces altars to this rapacious deity. But, what I find in reality is a warmth and generosity from groups of people who love to learn, have a similar liking for the world of art and antiques, and, in a way that is both comforting and accommodating, really want to join in. It's to all these people that I say thank you, from the bottom of my heart, for coming to all the events that I am asked to do – and likewise to the organisers and wonderful small bookshops that put in so much hard work to make these occasions happen, usually voluntarily and for small rewards. I enjoy it greatly; I also enjoy the other speakers that I encounter and think myself honoured to eat supper with erudite and charismatic characters like Terry Waite!

So, burgeoning fan base aside and notwithstanding my innate predilection and curiosity for the pursuit of the interesting, there would be literally no inspiration to write these books if it weren't for the venerable, disparate, nostalgic, pompous and bizarre order of the art and antiques world and the people who inhabit it. To them I owe a very big thank you too – from the auction houses that selflessly answer my searching enquiries and the various other accommodating colleagues that I regularly work with

Acknowledgements

in the auction world to my many colleagues on the *Antiques Roadshow* whose knowledge and expertise confounds and confirms my wayward analysis and hunches. Also, to my Series Editor Simon Shaw on what is undoubtedly one of the best British programmes ever to be devised and all the crew and colleagues that work on the show and make it such a great institution – many thanks.

Not forgetting some long-suffering people either: my wife Lisa, for one! A special thank you to my friend Valerie Singleton who always supports me in my literary endeavours. The editors who commission me to write for their magazines – I love the variety of this work – and finally to all the people on the ground at Icon Books that manage me and make it all happen: Leena, Stevie, Steve, Michael, Robert, Andrew, Nira, Duncan, Philip and Peter – many, many thanks.

PICTURE ACKNOWLEDGEMENTS

The Japanese mermaid image on page 54 comes courtesy of Corbis.

The illustration on page 77 is by Nicholas Halliday.

Thanks to the National Army Museum (www.nam.ac.uk) for the picture of Marengo's skeleton on page 90.

The photograph of Aleister Crowley on page 155 comes courtesy of the Press Association.

Cassini's *Carte de la Lune* on page 207 is reproduced courtesy of the Bibliothèque nationale de France.

BIBLIOGRAPHY

General resources
www.wikipedia.org
www.britannica.com
www.brainyquote.com
www.artprice.com

Sources regarding specific entries*
http://www.dailymail.co.uk/news/article-2931834/Lost-Constable
-sells-auction-3-5million-1-000-TIMES-went-just-18-months-ago
-experts-thought-work-copycat.html (Feeling Constable?)
http://www.bbc.co.uk/news/entertainment-arts-22626589 (Feeling
Constable?)
http://www.bbc.co.uk/news/uk-england-essex-30211588 (London
Calling)
http://forums.canadiancontent.net/history/65837-old-london-bridge
-1209-1831-a.html (London Calling)
http://hidden-london.com/the-guide/old-london-bridge/ (London
Calling)
http://greatwen.com/2011/04/14/secret-london-finding-bits-of-lost
-london-bridge/ (London Calling)
http://knowledgeoflondon.com/londonbridge.html/ (London Calling)
http://www.fromquarkstoquasars.com/meet-belka-and-strelka-the-frist
-earthlings-to-survive-orbital-flight/ (Dog On)
http://webecoist.momtastic.com/2011/04/05/bark-at-the-moon-a
-history-of-soviet-space-dogs/ (Dog On)

---

* Links correct at the time of writing.

Bibliography

http://www.nhm.ac.uk/about-us/news/2009/february/dogs-return-to
-gallery-in-museum-at-tring27259.html (Dog On)

http://www.nrm.org.uk/ (Dog On)

http://www.theguardian.com/artanddesign/2013/nov/08/cromwell
-portraitist-samuel-cooper-exhibition (Warts and All)

http://www.theguardian.com/politics/2014/nov/23/oliver-cromwell
-burial-plaque-sold-auction (Warts and All)

http://www.sothebys.com/en/auctions/ecatalogue/2013/english
-literature-history-l13404/lot.205.html (Warts and All)

http://www.archaeology.co.uk/blog/chris-catling/morris-and-the
-prince-the-battle-for-the-soul-of-trafalgar-square-stone-on-stone-and
-the-fifth-no-more-silly-walks-an-ancient-falcons-nest-and-other-tales
-of-longevity-how-many-skulls-did-oliver-cromw.htm (Warts and All)

http://www.thecourier.co.uk/news/local/angus-the-mearns/sale-of
-the-century-20-china-vase-and-bowl-sell-for-10-000-times-that-at
-montrose-auction-1.830577 (Black and White)

http://news.sky.com/story/1387244/holy-bargain-batmobile-sells-for
-90k (Holy Backfire)

http://www.1966batmobile.com/ (Holy Backfire)

http://www.batmobilehistory.com/barris-batmobile.php (Holy
Backfire)

http://www.ambergallery.com/Is_it_real_amber_/is_it_real_amber
_.html (Baltic Beauty)

https://www.bonhams.com/auctions/20027/lot/9/ (Jamaica Rum)

http://www.dailymail.co.uk/news/article-2843451/2p-Dinky-toys
-fetch-50-000-auction-Collection-12-rare-delivery-vans-1933-bought
-private-collector.html (Triumphant)

http://www.dnw.co.uk/auction-archive/catalogue-archive/lot.
php?auction_id=330&lot_id=107067 (Battle Orders)

http://www.dnw.co.uk/auction-archive/catalogue-archive/lot.php?
auction_id=330&lot_id=107065 (Battle Orders)

http://www.bonhams.com/auctions/22277/lot/152/ (Battle Orders)

http://www.christies.com/lotfinder/lot/an-extremely-rare-victorian
-novelty-mark-of-4757889-details.aspx?intObjectID=4757889
(Cock-a-Hoop)

http://www.garrickclub.co.uk/charitable_trust (Launch Night) http://www.theguardian.com/film/2001/mar/06/news (Launch Night)

http://www.bonhams.com/press_release/17545/ (Baby Doll)

http://collectdolls.about.com/od/fashiondolls/fl/Jumeau-201.htm (Baby Doll)

http://www.theguardian.com/music/2013/dec/06/bob-dylan-electric -guitar-fender-stratocaster-auction-christies (Black Beauty)

http://www.cbc.ca/news/world/les-paul-s-black-beauty-guitar-sells -for-419-900-1.2964597 (Black Beauty)

http://www.victoriacross.org.uk/vvashcro.htm (Subject Matters)

http://www.bbc.co.uk/news/uk-england-cornwall-31524625 (Skip Cat)

http://www.christies.com/features/Jerry_Garcia_Hat-5308-1.aspx (Hat Trick)

http://www.angelfire.com/wi/blindfaith/vvcov69.html (Space Odyssey)

http://www.nicholasbagshawe.com/view-artwork.asp?id=152 (Blind Vision)

http://www.oxfordtimes.co.uk/news/yourtown/oxford/11853300.Co in_auction_shows_how_to_turn___1_into___56_120/ (Pound for Pound)

http://www.dailymail.co.uk/news/article-2974559/Rare-1-coin-dates -English-Civil-War-passed-one-family-expected-fetch-50-000-auction .html (Pound for Pound)

http://www.woolleyandwallis.co.uk/Lot/?sale=AF080115&lot=554 &id=283307 (Freak Show)

http://www.gazettelive.co.uk/news/teesside-news/rare-star-wars-boba -fett-8534782 (Bounty Hunter)

http://www.jedinews.co.uk/news/news.aspx?newsID=18945 (Bounty Hunter)

http://www.telegraph.co.uk/culture/books/booknews/11149406/ Londons-literary-benches-fetch-high-sums-for-charity.html (Benchmark)

http://www.dailymail.co.uk/news/article-2219025/Book-auction -jackpot-Classic-edition-collection-including-James-Bond-Stephen -King-worth-millions-pensioner.html (Modern First)

Bibliography

http://www.bbc.co.uk/news/uk-england-northamptonshire-30428747 (Murder Most Horrid)

http://www.timelineauctions.com/lot/gilt-bronze-box-brooch-with-entwined-animals/40029/ (Burnt Cakes)

http://www.the-saleroom.com/en-gb/auction-catalogues/reeman-dansie/catalogue-id-srree10014/lot-c2984189-d479-405f-ae07-a43300f3847f (Indian Takeaway)

https://www.bonhams.com/auctions/16851/lot/366/ (Indian Takeaway)

http://www.orkney.gov.uk/OIC-News/stromness-museum-lahore.htm (Indian Takeaway)

http://collections.vam.ac.uk/item/O18891/maharaja-ranjit-singhs-throne-throne-chair-hafiz-muhammad/ (Indian Takeaway)

http://www.telegraph.co.uk/culture/art/art-news/10638011/Francis-Bacon-painting-breaks-records-after-42-million-sale.html (Bacon and Eggs)

http://www.harrogate-news.co.uk/2015/04/07/new-world-record-for-artist-norman-stansfield-cornish/ (Mum and Dad)

http://www.telegraph.co.uk/news/worldnews/europe/germany/11432544/Mummified-monk-revealed-inside-1000-year-old-Buddha-statue.html (Living Buddhas)

http://www.dailymail.co.uk/news/article-390834/Princess-Margaret-jewellery-flogging-vulgar.html (Right Royal)

http://www.roseberys.co.uk/calendar-and-catalogues/previous-auction-results/ (Love Tie)

http://news.sky.com/story/1249711/last-titanic-letter-fetches-record-price (From the Bridge)

http://militaryhistorynow.com/2014/05/16/military-history-in-100-objects-giddy-up-famous-stuffed-war-horses/ (Horse Play)

http://www.walesonline.co.uk/news/local-news/remarkable-charge-light-brigade-warhorse-2013021 (Horse Play)

http://www.soane.org/opening-up-the-soane/phase-ii-soanes-private-apartments/the-model-room/ (Temple of Delights)

http://www.sworder.co.uk/index.php?_a=viewProd&productId=80057 (Temple of Delights)

http://www.coulborn.com/furniture-categories/notable-sales/cork
-model-of-the-temple-of-poseidon-now-thought-to-be-of-zeus-at
-paestum/ (Temple of Delights)

http://www.christies.com/lotfinder/lot/an-18k-gold-lapis-lazuli-and-
coral-4911249-details.aspx?intObjectID=4911249 (Bird in the Hand)

http://iantiqueonline.ning.com/forum/topics/fontaines-sets-its-6th
-world (Wheels of Industry)

http://www.theguardian.com/world/2014/mar/27/sevso-treasure
-items-repatriated-hungarian-government-roman-silver (Roman Riches)

http://ottawacitizen.com/news/national/franklin-expedition-medal-for
-sale (Poles Apart II)

http://www.christies.com/features/Art_Object_4-5365-1.aspx (Poles
Apart II)

http://hidden-tracks-book.blogspot.co.uk/2010/05/lt-irving-memorial
.html (Poles Apart II)

http://www.bbc.co.uk/news/uk-england-stoke-staffordshire-29460282
(Black Basalt)

http://www.christies.com/lotfinder/lot/an-english-delft-dated-blue
-dash-royal-portrait-5323478-details.aspx (Royal Mug)

http://www.scribd.com/doc/30827576/Seduction-of-the-Innocent
-1954-2nd-Printing#scribd (Piano Lesson)

http://collections.vam.ac.uk/item/O140531/costume-design-by-ronald
-cobb-costume-design-cobb-ronald/ (Burlesque Beauties)

http://www.shadyoldlady.com/location.php?loc=2220 (Burlesque
Beauties)

http://ngmaindia.gov.in/sh-company-period.asp (Two's Company)

http://www.history.com/topics/kamehameha-iv (Feather Boa)

http://www.timelineauctions.com/lot/king-robert-the-bruce-of-
scotland-and-dunfermline-abbey-cokete-seal-ma/40004/ (Braveheart)

http://www.telegraph.co.uk/news/worldnews/europe/france
/11237306/Revealed-The-chicken-mogul-who-bought-Napoleons-hat
-for-1.5-million.html (Bicorn or Tricorn)

http://www.dailymail.co.uk/news/article-2314292/A-cracking-sale
-Elephant-egg-ONE-HUNDRED-times-bigger-hens-egg-goes-66-000.
html (Sunny Side Up)

Bibliography

http://www.tate.org.uk/art/artworks/long-river-avon-mud-drawings
-ten-mud-dipped-papers-ar00616 (Mud Bath)

http://www.thecityreview.com/f04scon2.html (Scrap Heap)

http://www.hermanmiller.com/products/tables/occasional-tables/
noguchi-table.html (Scrap Heap)

http://www.cigaraficionado.com/webfeatures/show/id/A-Gentleman
-of-History_6006/ (Churchill's Crown)

http://www.irishexaminer.com/ireland/native-american-outfit-sells-for
-euro320k-in-kilkenny-314742.html (American Beauty)

http://www.pullmangallery.com/cat/51/Alfred-Dunhill-Lighters
(Budgie Smuggler)

http://www.sothebys.com/en/auctions/2015/bear-witness-l15026.ht
ml#&page=all&sort=lotNum-asc&viewMode=list&lot=1&scroll
=1300 (Bear Witness)

http://www.telegraph.co.uk/news/picturegalleries/uknews
/11450954/Bear-Witness-Sothebys-auction-strange-collection
-including-paintings-and-skulls.html?frame=3220387 (Bear Witness)

http://www.pbase.com/cameramanuk/image/99979993 (Yellow
Midget)

http://camerapedia.wikia.com/wiki/Coronet_Midget (Yellow Midget)

http://collections.vam.ac.uk/item/O70347/the-emperor-rudolph-ii
-bust-vries-adriaen-de/ (Weight of the World)

https://www.rijksmuseum.nl/en/press/press-releases/rijksmuseum
-acquires-masterpiece-by-the-sculptor-adriaen-de-vries (Weight of
the World)

http://www.antiquestradegazette.com/news/2013/jun/06/victorian
-whalebone-cane-takes-27000/ (Stick Shift)

http://www.independent.co.uk/news/people/phial-of-winston
-churchills-blood-withdrawn-from-sale-at-auction-10103315.html
(Blood is Thicker)

http://www.bbc.co.uk/news/uk-england-oxfordshire-32750247 (Arms
House)

http://www.dreweatts.com/cms/pages/lots/19204?auction-id=2998&
lots.~rsp.p=3&lots.~rsp.gp=4&currency=&lots.~rsp.l=20&lots.~
rsp.cl=20&lots.~rsp.ss=date%2Ca&lots.~rsp.css=number%2Ca
(Black Magic)

Bibliography

http://www.reuters.com/article/2015/01/07/us-usa-massachusetts
-time-capsule-idUSKBN0KF11320150107 (Time Team)

http://boston.cbslocal.com/2014/12/11/crews-work-to-extract
-1795-time-capsule-from-state-house/ (Time Team)

http://www.mirror.co.uk/news/weird-news/gandalfs-staff-lord-rings
-sells-4544120 (Ring-a-Ding)

http://www.theguardian.com/world/2014/nov/27/stuart-little-art
-historian-long-lost-hungarian-masterpiece?CMP=share_btn_tw
(Out of Time)

http://www.bbc.co.uk/news/entertainment-arts-30467820 (Out of Time)

http://www.dailymail.co.uk/news/article-3040676/Sex-toy-18th
-Century-discovered-archaeologists-ancient-Polish-training-arena
-swordsmen.html (Cock Up)

http://news.discovery.com/history/archaeology/18th-century-sex-toy
-found-in-ancient-latrine-150415.htm (Cock Up)

http://artsbeat.blogs.nytimes.com/2015/03/25/a-painting-sold-by-the
-met-is-declared-a-true-rubens/?_r=0 (Real or No Real)

https://news.artnet.com/art-world/metropolitan-museum-castoff-is
-real-rubens-281609 (Real or No Real)

http://www.christies.com/lotfinder/drawings-watercolors/sir-peter
-paul-rubens-two-nude-5868569-details.aspx (Real or No Real)

http://www.telegraph.co.uk/luxury/art/60428/market-news-a-new
-london-record.html (Real or No Real)

http://www.christies.com/lotfinder/watches/attributed-to-freres
-rochat-the-only-5448775-details.aspx (Mechanical Marvel)

http://www.sothebys.com/en/auctions/ecatalogue/2015/treasures
-l15303/lot.47.html (Mechanical Marvel)

http://www.sothebys.com/en/auctions/2013/treasures-princely-taste
-l13303.html (Mechanical Marvel)

http://www.sothebys.com/content/sothebys/en/auctions/ecatalogue
/2015/watches-n09368/lot.114.html (Mechanical Marvel)

http://blog.britishmuseum.org/2015/04/17/conservation-of-a-clove
-boat/ (Spice Trade)

http://www.paulfrasercollectibles.com/news/movie-memorabilia/
marilyn-monroes-grave-marker-to-surpass-4-000/19590.page (Silver
Screen Siren)

Bibliography

http://www.paulfrasercollectibles.com/news/vivien-leighs-gone-with
-the-wind-dress-realises-137-000/19365.page?catid=26 (Going,
Going, Gone)

http://janetteheffernan.blogspot.co.uk/2011/12/my-favorite-elizabeth
-taylor-jewels.html (Just the Ticket)

http://www.woolleyandwallis.co.uk/Lot/?sale=JW220115&lot=1242&
id=286248 (Just the Ticket)

http://www.dailymail.co.uk/news/article-2211004/Bonnie-Clyde
-auction-Pistols-owned-criminals-sell-500K.html (Gangster Rap)

http://www.lettersofnote.com/2009/12/what-dandy-car-you-make
.html (Gangster Rap)

http://www.whiskybible.com/index.html (A Wee Dram)

http://www.wine-searcher.com/find/suntory+the+yamazaki+sherry+
cask+single+malt+whisky+japan (A Wee Dram)

http://www.telegraph.co.uk/news/uknews/crime/11700605/Holy
-Grail-found-by-police-in-Herefordshire.html (Holy Hoaxes)

http://www.newquay-westwales.co.uk/strata_florida.htm (Holy
Hoaxes)

http://auctions.lyonandturnbull.com/auction-lot-detail/A-pair-of
-gold-mounted-musket-balls/429++++++122+/++193611 (Muzzle
Loader)

http://www.sothebys.com/en/auctions/ecatalogue/2011/african
-oceanic-and-precolumbian-art-n08749/lot.306.html (Narcotics Bust)

http://fijiguide.com/page/4351878:Page:55 (Narcotics Bust)

http://www.specialauctionservices.com/large/me250215/page013.
html (Record Record)

http://www.christies.com/lotfinder/paintings/cy-twombly-untitled
-5846075-details.aspx (Blackboard Scribble)

http://www.artnews.com/2014/11/12/christies-contemporary-art-sale
-nets-853-9-m-all-time-auction-record/ (Blackboard Scribble)

http://www.bbc.co.uk/news/magazine-27903742 (Flayed Alive!)

http://www.dailymail.co.uk/news/article-3140836/Napoleon-s-hat-set
-sell-500-000-complete-bullet-mark-shot-wearing-it.html (Newsflash)

https://www.justcollecting.com/militaria/napoleons-hat-could-bring
-500-000-at-christies-extraordinary-sale (Newsflash)

https://www.justcollecting.com/militaria/historic-wwii-spitfire-set-for
-2-5-million-charity-sale-at-christies (Newsflash)

http://www.esa.int/About_Us/Welcome_to_ESA/ESA_history/Jean
-Dominique_Cassini_Astrology_to_astronomy (Lunar Love)

http://www.bonhams.com/auctions/22386/#/aao=15&MR0_length
=10&wo=list&mo=0 (Freeze Dried)

http://www.artnews.com/2012/01/12/american-art-alice-walton
%E2%80%99s-way/ (American Realist)

http://www.bbc.co.uk/news/uk-england-32294655 (An Enigma)

http://www.christies.com/lotfinder/sculptures-statues-figures/
demetre-h-chiparus-semiramis-a-cold-painted-and-5085983-details
.aspx (Ivory Queen)

http://www.ncbi.nlm.nih.gov/pubmed/23798048 (Gottle o' Geer)

http://www.bbc.co.uk/news/uk-england-shropshire-33122420 (Gottle
o' Geer)

http://www.christies.com/lotfinder/lot/an-important-nanban-six-fold
-screen-depicting-the-5894145-details.aspx (Barbarian Hordes)

https://togeii.wordpress.com/2010/02/05/what-is-nanban/ (Barbarian
Hordes)

http://www.indepcndent.co.uk/property/house-and-home/rare-wood
-sparks-buying-frenzy-in-china-2296824.html (Woodn't it be Nice)

http://www.huffingtonpost.com/2013/01/17/gold-nugget-australia
-ballarat-found_n_2496663.html (Scraps of Knowledge)

http://m.oxfordmail.co.uk/news/top_news/13360119.Couple_discove
r_lost_Constable_drawing/?ref=mac (Feeling Less Constable)

http://www.bbc.co.uk/news/uk-england-26469589 (Feeling Less
Constable)

http://www.christies.com/lotfinder/lot/a-vincennes-porcelain-blue
-lapis-teapot-and-5715820-details.aspx (Sèvres You Right)

http://www.adriansassoon.com/antique/early-vincennes?view=
artwork&id=1703 (Sèvres You Right)

http://www.christies.com/lotfinder/lot/a-vincennes-porcelain-blue
-lapis-teapot-and-5715820-details.aspx (Sèvres You Right)

http://www.adriansassoon.com/antique/early-vincennes?view=
artwork&id=1703 (Sèvres You Right)

Bibliography

http://www.outdoorhub.com/stories/2015/07/02/10-expensive
-notorious-guns-world/ (High Calibre)

http://www.usatoday.com/story/news/nation/2014/04/18/wyatt
-earp-guns-auction/7868943/ (High Calibre)

http://www.buffalobill.org/ (High Calibre)

https://www.justcollecting.com/miscellania/buffalo-bills-remington
-revolver-may-bring-200-000-to-wild-west-auction (High Calibre)

http://www.dailymail.co.uk/news/article-2659216/Buffalo-Bills
-necklace-gun-fetch-80K-auction.html (High Calibre)

http://www.codydugupgunmuseum.com/ (High Calibre)

http://www.9news.com/story/news/local/storytellers/2015/01/02/
buffalo-bill-death/21191731/ (Grave Thought)

http://www.findagrave.com/cgi-bin/fg.cgi?GRid=211&page=gr
(Grave Thought)

https://www.bonhams.com/auctions/15273/lot/88/ (Drink Up)

http://www.telegraph.co.uk/luxury/design/66382/newsons-lockheed
-an-icon-up-for-auction.html (Design for Life)

http://www.dezeen.com/2015/04/29/marc-newson-lockheed-lounge
-new-auction-record-design-object-phillips/ (Design for Life)

http://www.telegraph.co.uk/news/uknews/11502701/Charles-Dickens
-desk-saved-for-the-nation.html (What the Dickens)

http://news.bbc.co.uk/1/hi/entertainment/7435167.stm (What the
Dickens)

http://www.christies.com/presscenter/pdf/04022008/101339.pdf
(What the Dickens)

http://www.sothebys.com/en/auctions/ecatalogue/2015/antiquities
-n09362/lot.41.html (Attic Find)

http://www.christies.com/lotfinder/books-manuscripts/a-kufic-quran
-folio-on-blue-vellum-5551207-details.aspx (Persian Perfection)

http://www.sothebys.com/en/auctions/ecatalogue/2015/arts-islamic
-world-l15220/lot.61.html (Persian Perfection)

http://www.rugkazbah.com/boards/records.php?id=2652&refnum
=2652 (Flat Weave)

http://www.christies.com/features/Mongol-Textile-5861-1.aspx (Flat
Weave)

Bibliography

http://www.dailymail.co.uk/news/article-3043355/The-spoils-Empire
-Bounty-looted-Wellington-s-men-defeated-Tiger-Mysore-s-Indian
-palace-set-sell-1million.html (Mysore Magic)

http://www.sothebys.com/en/auctions/ecatalogue/2013/art-imperial
-india-l13502/lot.249.html (Mysore Magic)

http://www.sundaypost.com/news-views/scotland/metal-detector
-enthusiast-on-a-1-million-hot-streak-1.623567 (Field Find)

http://www.bbc.co.uk/news/uk-england-somerset-32992960 (Field
Find)

http://www.antiquebottles.co.za/pages/categories/CoddPatents.htm
(Lots of Bottle)

http://onlinebbr.com/ (Lots of Bottle)

http://www.abc.net.au/news/2012-06-03/tintin-cover-fetches-record
-price/4049036 (Just One Drink)

http://www.christies.com/Tintin-25890.aspx (Just One Drink)

http://www.inprint.co.uk/thebookguide/shops/good_bye_sambo.php
(Slave Trader)

http://www.antiquesyoungguns.co.uk/our-blogs/a-slice-of
-transatlantic-communication-history--496.html (Cable Tie)

http://atlantic-cable.com/Article/Lanello/ (Cable Tie)

http://atlantic-cable.com//Cableships/GreatEastern/ (Cable Tie)

http://atlantic-cable.com/Cables/1854-57Mediterranean/ (Cable Tie)

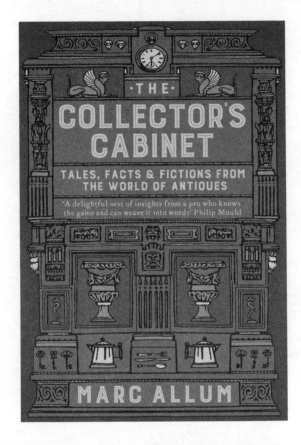